MW01231931

Day

of

Reckoning

by

David Arnold

ISBN- 13:978-1522893813
ISBN- 10:1522893814

Acknowledgements

Thank you to my wife, Linda, for her many hours of reading, critiquing, and editing. Thank you to my family for their continued support for my writings.

Table of Contents

Day of Reckoning

Introduction

When President Dwight Eisenhower was vacationing in Denver, he was told about Paul Haley, a six- year-old boy who was dying of an incurable cancer. Paul had one big desire – to someday meet the president of the United States. To one of his aides, President Eisenhower said, "Let's go see him." With flags flying on that August Sunday afternoon, the black limousine drove up to the Haley home. Paul and his family had no idea that Eisenhower was coming. The president stepped out with his bodyguards and knocked on the door. Paul's father answered, wearing old blue jeans, an old dirty shirt, sporting a full day's growth of his beard. "Can I help ya?" he asked. The President responded, "Is Paul here? Tell him the President of the United States would like to meet him." Little Paul, amazed and thrilled, walked around his father's legs, stood and looked into the face of the man he most admired. Eisenhower knelt down, shook his hand, and took him out to see the presidential limousine. Before leaving, he hugged little Paul. They shook hands again, then, just as suddenly as he appeared – he was gone.

The neighbors still talk about that day. But one man was not entirely happy about it, and that was Paul's dad, Donald Haley. He said, "I'll never forget standing there in those old jeans, a dirty shirt and a grubby beard, to meet the president. If only I'd known he was coming!"[1] Hebrews 9:8, "Christ will appear a second time…to those who are [eagerly, constantly, and patiently] waiting for and expecting Him" (The Amplified Bible).

In Matthew 24:37, Christ said, "But as the days of Noah were, so also will the coming of the Son of Man be." What He meant was that Noah lived in a world that was a carbon copy of the hour we live. By following the footsteps of Noah's society, it will lead us to our generation. The last civilization will end like the first. Our world will follow the same path… a world that is rushing headlong towards judgment, step by step. The people of Noah's time had their day of reckoning. Likewise, there is coming another day of reckoning. The Bible warns, "I saw the small and great, standing before God, and the books were opened…And they were judged, each one according to his works" (Revelation 20:12).

From the Scriptures, we discover five descriptions of Noah's day. Each is a photo of the generation which will experience the Second Coming of Christ. These five descriptions are:

The Attitude of Those Days
(Genesis 6:1 – 13)

The Actions of Those Days
(Matthew 24)

The Apathy of Those Days
(Matthew 25:1 - 13)

The Apostasy of Those Days
(Romans 1:18 – 32))

The Arranging for Those Days
(Hebrews 11:7))

Chapter One

The Attitude of Those Days

(Genesis 6:1 – 13)

"We need to understand that the return of Jesus Christ – the Second Advent – is a major Biblical doctrine. We neglect it at our peril. As Dr. Wilbur Smith reminds us, 'There are many, many prophecies in the Old and New Testaments regarding the end of the age and our Lord's return.' To become alarmed over the trend of events in our time, one does not need to be pessimistic. Just to be observant and honest is enough to tell one that pre-flood conditions have, in good part, returned. Jesus said, 'As it was, so shall it be.' Those conditions which prevailed in antediluvian days will be fulfilled again in the last days before the return of Jesus Christ."[1]

In Genesis 6:1 – 13, the Scriptures reveal the following about the attitude of the days of Noah: the attitude of society, the attitude of God, and the attitude of Noah. It is a full account of the world's degeneracy and rebellion against God. The destroying of it was an act of necessary justice for the maintaining of the honor of God's government.

The Attitude of Society

In Matthew 24:3 and 12, Christ, when asked about "the sign of Your coming and of the end (the completion, the consummation) of the age," He described society as one of "multiplied lawlessness and iniquity." "Iniquity" means "illegality, violation of the law, wickedness, unrighteousness, lawless, transgression, and unrighteousness."[2] A man entered a tailor shop and requested that he get a suit made in one week's time. He needed it for an important function. The tailor told him that he must take at least three weeks to make a new suit. "Three weeks," echoed the man. "What do you mean three weeks? God created the whole world in seven days, and you need three weeks to make a suit?" "True enough," answered the tailor. "God created the entire world in seven days and look at the way it looks."[3]

There was pluralism, a mixture of the godly with the ungodly. "Now it came to pass, when men began to multiply on the face of the earth, and daughters were born to them, that the sons of God saw the daughters of men, that they were beautiful; and they took wives for themselves of all whom they chose" (vv. 1, 2). The increase of people on the earth was the effect of the blessing of God (Genesis 1:28), and yet man's corruption so abused and perverted this blessing that it was turned into a curse. Proverbs 29:16 tells us, "When the wicked are multiplied, transgression increases." The more sinners, the more sin, and as offenders multiply, men are embolden in their wickedness. Infectious diseases are most deadly in populous cities, and sin is a spreading virus. "The sons of God," that is, the people of God, married the "daughters of men," those who did not serve God. The descendants of Seth did not marry their own, but intermarried with the ungodly.

They made their choices only by the eye, "The sons of God saw the daughters of men, that they were beautiful." Further, they followed their own affection, "...of all whom they chose." Such actions were strictly forbidden to Israel, "Nor shall you make marriages with them...for they will turn your sons away from following Me, to serve other gods (Deuteronomy 7:3, 4). This was the unhappy occasion for Solomon's apostasy (1 Kings 11:1 – 4), for we read, "When Solomon was old, his wives turned his heart after other gods; and his heart was not loyal to the Lord his God." It was also a bad consequence of the Jews after their return from Babylon (Ezra 9:1, 2). A German proverb says, "When a dove begins to associate with a crow its feathers remain white, but its heart grows black."[4] The bad will sooner contaminate the good than the good reform the bad. This mixture between the godly and the ungodly resulted in a loss of the worship of Jehovah God and the compromise of absolute truth... until anything and all things were accepted.

.*"Pluralism" is a philosophy that says that different religions are just different routes to God.* Let's all join together, because we're all headed in the same direction. A commentary appeared in a major United States newspaper entitled, "Pluralism May Close the Gap Among Faiths." It stated, "Pluralism frequently compels individuals to acknowledge that there are various ways to achieve a spiritually fulfilling life. While all religions are true for their believers, *pluralism teaches that no one religion contains all the truth for everyone throughout the world.*"[5] In

Revelation 17, we have a vivid description of the religion of the last day. This religious mindset is pictured as having "a golden cup." The "golden cup" is one cup. All the religions of the world will come together and drink from the same cup, as the world promotes pluralism. However, this deception is doomed from the outset, because the writer, John, is told, "Come, and I will show you the doom (sentence, judgment) of the great harlot who sits on many waters" (Revelation 17:1). Such is the future of all those who reject the claim of Christ in John 14:6, "I am the Way, the Truth and the Life; no one comes to the Father except by (through) Me" (The Amplified Bible).

There was contempt. "There were giants on the earth in those days, and also afterward, when the sons of God came in to the daughters of men and they bore children to them. Those were mighty men who were of old, men of renown" (v. 4). "Giants" speak of those who were tyrants, the backslidden, fallen ones, roving, lawless ones who attack others, as do robbers or the malicious. "Renown" speaks of those who boast of their wickedness, oppression, violence, unashamed of sin. These were oppressive, influential men who led people to sin, and trampled upon all that were just and sacred, holding righteousness and godliness in contempt.

"Woe to those who drag their sins behind them like a bullock on a rope. They even mock the Holy One of Israel and dare the Lord to punish them" (Isaiah 5:18, 19 – The Living Bible). Isaiah is describing those who do not innocently fall into sin, but consciously choose evil over righteousness. They draw it to themselves, seek after it, and willingly commit it. Further, they lust for and solicit all opportunities of doing it, while making use of all arguments, reasonings, and deceit to engage themselves and others in the practice of it. So intoxicated with seeking sinful pleasure, they shut God out of their lives. When confronted with their sin, instead of being convicted, they accuse others of being "holier-than-thou," and even defy God.

"Sin is man's declaration of independence of God."[6] W. B. Yeats tells of Lionel Johnson, the scholar and poet. Johnson was an alcoholic. He had, as he said himself, "...a craving that made every atom of his body cry out." But, when it was suggested that he should undergo treatment to overcome this craving, his answer quite frankly was, "I do not want to be cured."[7]

There was corruption. "Every intent of the thoughts of his heart was only evil continually" (v. 5b). "The earth also was corrupt before God, and the earth was filled with violence" (v. 11). "And indeed it was corrupt; for all flesh had corrupted their way on the earth" (v. 12b). "And God said to Noah, 'The end of all flesh has come before Me, for the earth is filled with violence through them; and behold, I will destroy them with the earth'" (v. 13). The word "thoughts" is also translated "imagination." The word "image" is found in imagination, for it represents the pictures we allow to come to the eyes of our hearts. The word "corrupt" is referred to three times and "violence" twice. "Corrupt" means "to decay and ruin." "Violence" means

14

"cruelty, injustice, wrong, to maltreat, violated, shake off, imagine wrongfully (mental violence)."[8] There were no limits to the moral deviancy of man. Every abomination imaginable (and unimaginable) had become the lifestyle.

Isaiah wrote, "But the wicked are like the troubled sea, when it cannot rest, whose waters cast up mire and dirt" (Isaiah 57:20). "Mire" and "dirt!" That is the toxic condition of mankind at this juncture. Not only is there a flood of moral filth, corruption has spread into every area of life. The words of Isaiah are carefully chosen by the Holy Spirit, "...like the troubled sea." There is agitation, violence, and immorality worldwide. "Mankind has known intuitively for at least 50 centuries that indiscriminate sexual activity represents both an individual and a corporate threat to survival. And history bears it out. Anthropologist J. D. Unwin conducted an exhaustive study of the 88 civilizations which have existed in the history of the world. Each culture has reflected a similar life cycle, beginning with a strict code of sexual conduct and ending with the demand for complete 'freedom' to express individual passion. Unwin reports that every society which extended sexual permissiveness to its people was soon to perish. There have been no exceptions."[9]

The Attitude of God

Victor Hugo gave a marvelous description of Waterloo. It is one of the masterpieces of all literature. In that description, he asks, "Was it possible for Napoleon to win at Waterloo? No.

Because of Wellington? No. Because of Blucher? No. Because of rain? No. Then why was it impossible for Napoleon to win at Waterloo?" "Because of God," answers Hugo, and then continues with something of the touch of sacrilege, as he added, "Napoleon bothered God." Woe be to that generation that bothers God![10]

In Psalm 82:8, the psalmist cries, "Arise, O God, judge the earth." This is a metaphor from the common gesture of judges whose usual habit is to sit while they are hearing a case. Then, they arise and stand up when they are ready to give sentence. There are four actions taken by God.

He made a decision (v. 3). This is His token of displeasure at what they had done. He resolved, "My Spirit will not always strive with man forever."

1 Peter 3:20 and 2 Peter 2:5 explains that the Holy Spirit spoke to them through Noah's preaching and by inward checks, but it was in vain with the most of them, though God patiently waited. Then He decided that His Spirit would not always abide or dwell with man forever. According to Hosea 4:17, if the Spirit is resisted, quenched, and striven against, though He pleads and warns long, He will not do so always. On the banks of the Niagara, where the rapids begin to swell and swirl most violently in preparation for their final plunge, is a signboard which bears the following sign: "Past Redemption Point." Even while one feels the firm ground beneath his feet, a severe warning grips the person's heart, as he looks off into the turbulent waters, and realizes the full significance of the sign, "Past

Redemption Point."[11] His reason was, "For he is indeed flesh." They had become so incurably corrupt, carnal, and sensual that the striving of the Spirit was useless. His reprieve was, "Yet his days shall be one hundred and twenty years." God announces a definite term of rebellion – 120 years. His patience is sometimes long, but it is limited – reprieves are not pardons Psalm 97:3 states, "A fire goes before Him" …like a marshal or advance guard before a royal presence. Fire is the sign both of grace and wrath. God marches forth in both displays of Deity.

He did a thorough investigation. "Then the Lord saw that the wickedness of man was great in the earth" (v. 5a)… "So God looked upon the earth" (v. 12a). Twice, it states that He was an eyewitness, for He "saw" and "looked."

The evidence for His investigation was incontestable. He saw their actions and their hearts. The stream of sin was full, and strong, and constant, and God personally scrutinized it. Psalm 14:2, 3, "The Lord looks down from heaven on all mankind to see if there are any who are wise, who want to please God. But no, all have strayed away; all are rotten with sin. Not one is good, not one!" (The Living Bible)

He revealed His emotions, "And the Lord was sorry that He had made man on the earth, and He was grieved in His heart" (v. 6). The German poet, Goethe, said, "If I were God, sin would break my heart."[12] This expresses His just and holy displeasure against sin and the sinful. He was injured, grieved, and displeased. Further expressions are used to define how the sin of man affects Him. He is grieved, wearied, crushed, and weighed down by the sins of His creation (Psalm 95:10; Isaiah 43:24; Ezekiel 6:9; Amos 2:13). As a parent is heartbroken over a wayward child, so is the heart of God grieved over wayward and sinful man. One of the marks of personality is feeling; if God did not feel grief, He would be imperfect in His love. Interestingly enough is to note that God was sorry that He made man, but we never find Him sorry that He redeemed man (though that was a work of much greater expense!).

He pronounced His verdict. "So the Lord said, 'I will destroy man whom I have created from the face of the earth, both man and beast, creeping thing and birds of the air, for I am sorry that I have made them'" (v. 7). "And God said to Noah, 'The end of all flesh has come before Me, for the earth is filled with violence through them; and behold, I will destroy them with the earth'" (v. 13). J. Oswald Sanders wrote, "When wickedness develops into extraordinary proportions, God meets it with extraordinary measures."[13] "Destroy" refers to dirt or filth wiped off a plate which should be clean, and thrown into the garbage in its proper place. Also, those lines which displease the author are deleted out of a book. Further, as a name of a citizen is removed from the rolls when he is dead or disfranchised. Man even used the animals by corrupting them with their abominations. This is why God destroyed the animals, too. Isaiah 27:11, "They are a foolish nation, a witless, stupid people, for they turn away from God. Therefore, He who made them will not have pity on them or show them His mercy" (The Living Bible). He refers to man as His own creature, even when He resolved to destroy him ("whom I have created"). Though He made man, He would not excuse him. God pronounced His verdict only after His Spirit had been long striving with man in vain. "Those forfeit their lives that do not answer the end of their living...None are ruined by the justice of God, but those that hate to be reformed by the grace of God."[14]

Years ago, a major news organization reported on an unusual work of modern art – a chair affixed to a shotgun. It was to be viewed by sitting in the chair and looking directly into the gun-barrel. The gun was loaded and set on a timer to fire at an unknown moment within the next 100 years. The shocking thing was that people waited in lines to sit and stare into the shell's path! They all knew that the gun could go off at point-blank range during their minute in the chair. How foolhardy, we exclaim, yet people who would never consider sitting in that chair live a lifetime gambling that they can get away with sin. Foolishly, they ignore the risk unto inevitable self-destruction.[15] "For he who sows to his own flesh (lower nature, sensuality) will from the flesh reap decay and ruin and destruction" (Galatians 6:8, The Amplified Bible).

The Attitude of Noah

Noah is mentioned by name five times in verses 8 – 10. He distinguished himself from the rest of the world and God honored him for it.

In his book, *Follow Thou Me*, the late

George W. Truett gave a word of warning relevant to all generations: "With many people, the chief standard of greatness is financial. The greatly honored and late Chief Justice of the Nation, the Honorable William Howard Taft, sounded a most timely admonition to the Nation, to the effect that the enthronement of the spirit of materialism in the fabric of our country's life contributes the most serious menace to our civilization and the security of our Republic. The true wealth of a country is not financial and material, but moral and spiritual. Civilization is a dismal failure, even though its banks be glutted with deposits, and its ships of commerce traverse all the seas, unless the true appraisement of human life shall be at the apex of such civilization. 'Ill fares the land, to hastening ills a prey, where

wealth accumulates and men decay.'
When Tennyson wrote his *Crossing the
Bar*, he did more for the making of a
stable, worthy civilization than if he had
built a thousand of the most splendid
ocean liners that ever ploughed the seas.
Verily, the financial standard, powerful
and important as it is, is not the chief
standard of greatness."[16]

He had favor with God. "But Noah
found grace in the eyes of the Lord" (v.
8). This is the first time "grace" is
mentioned in Scripture. "Grace" speaks
of "favor," or "acceptance." When
beholding the wicked, we read only that
He "saw" and "looked." A "look" was
sufficient to see the wickedness of men.
However, when Noah is in view, the
"eyes of the Lord" are mentioned. This
speaks of something more definite and
protracted. This was God's love and

mercy in action. He found grace, not because he earned it, but because he faithfully kept what had been given him, both through his ancestors and by the work of the Holy Spirit in his life. There was no grace in Noah; the grace was in the eyes of the Lord. When God extended grace to Noah, this signified that there was new life and new hope for mankind in the future. God was displeased with the rest of the world, but He showed His favor and acceptance to Noah. He had strictly examined the character of every person in the world before He pronounced it universally corrupt. However, when God examined Noah's heart, He found a man intent on walking with Him. Noah probably did not find favor in the eyes of men – they most likely hated and persecuted him, because both his life and preaching "passed judgment and sentence on the world's unbelief" (Hebrews 11:7). A. W. Tozer declared, "Before there can be acceptable service, there must be an acceptable life."[17] Noah's life was one acceptable to God in a world that had rejected Him.

He had a heart for God (vv. 9, 10). While the rest of the world was corrupt and wicked, Noah kept his integrity. "This is the genealogy of Noah" means "this is the account we have to give of him." He "was a just man." Noah was justified before God by faith in His promised seed. He lived by right principles, and was righteous in his living. "Just" means "straightness, uprightness, honest, virtuous, and pious" in behavior. He lived a life of moral and ethical righteousness. The word means that he conformed to a higher standard –

God's. He was "perfect in his generations." He remained uncontaminated in the midst corruption. "Perfect" speaks of one who is complete. Not sinlessness, but moral integrity. He was perfect in the sense that his heart was right with God. Note the words, "...in his generations." "Generations" means "age." Among his contemporaries, Noah stood out, for they lacked these qualities. This is what crowns his character. He was not a man whose character was shaped by the age in which he lived. He lived for God when no one else did. It is easy to be religious when religion is popular. But it is evidence of a strong faith to swim against popular opinion when being ridiculed and mocked. "Noah walked with God." Noah and his great-grandfather, Enoch, are the two men, before the flood, who are said to have walked with God, demonstrating that it is possible to walk with God in the midst of unbelief and rebellion. He was honest and devout. He acted with God.

The Hebrew reads, "With God, Noah did walk." His walk was with his God. His life deeply influenced his sons, "And Noah begat three sons: Shem, Ham, and Japheth" (v. 10). By following directly upon the statement of his devotion to God, the object is to remind the readers of the effect Noah's godly life must have had on his sons.

He received direction and deliverance, "And God said to Noah, 'The end of all flesh has come before Me, for the earth is filled with violence through them; and behold, I will destroy them with the earth'" (v. 13). God made him the man of His counsel and communication. He told him, in general, His plans (v. 13), then told him, in particular, what was to happen (vv. 14 – 22). Later, God told Abraham of His decision concerning Sodom, "Shall I hide from Abraham what I am doing?" (Genesis18:17) He did the same for Noah. Psalm 25:14, "The secret of the Lord is with those who fear Him, and He will show them His covenant." According to Amos 3:7, by a spirit of revelation, "He reveals His secret to His servants, the prophets," meaning that He informs them particularly of His purpose.

Billy Graham, in his book, *World Aflame*, describes the complacency of our times: "In a declining culture, one of its characteristics is that ordinary people are unaware of what is happening. Only those who know and can read the signs of decadence are posing the questions that as yet have no answer. Mr. Average Man is comfortable in his complacency, and is as unconcerned as a silverfish in a carton of discarded magazines on world affairs. He is not asking any questions, because his social benefits from the government give him a false sense of security. This is his trouble and his tragedy. Modern man has become a spectator of world events, observing on his television screen without becoming involved. He watches the ominous events of our times pass before his eyes, while he sips his beer in a comfortable chair. He does not seem to realize what is happening to him. He does not understand that his world is on fire, and he about to be burned up with it."[18]

"Though the patience of God be lasting, yet it is not *everlasting*" (William Secher).[19]

Chapter Two

The Actions of Those Days

(Matthew 24)

In a small southern town, a simple, aged lady came to do her shopping. Two or three young ruffians were standing around passing the time of day, and knowing she was a Christian, they began to taunt her. "We hear you're expecting Jesus to come back," they sarcastically asked. "I sure am," she brightly replied. "Do you really believe He's coming?" they asked with a smirk. "Sure as you were born," she answered. They said, "Well, you'd better hurry home and get ready, He might be on the way!" She turned and fixed her tormentors with a look. "I don't have to get ready," she said, "I *keep* ready!"[1]

In Matthew 24:37, Jesus clearly said, "But as the days of Noah were, so also will the coming of the Son of Man be." The days of Noah closed an era with judgment. So will the second coming of Christ close this era. He will put a period on time.

In chapter 24 of Matthew, we have revealed:

The Actions of the Father

The Actions of Society

The Actions of Believers

The Actions of the Father

There are three actions that God the Father will take on the day of Christ's return. First, it is a day of secrecy, for Christ stated, "But of that day and hour no one knows, no, not even the angels of heaven, but My Father only" (v. 36). "Of that day and hour" mean "of that precise time of fulfillment." The hour of that event is known to God, and to God alone. The wisest are ignorant of it, and the best minds will never discover it. It is a *certain* day and a *fixed* hour, for Christ spoke of "that day" and "that hour." The expression plainly implies that a definite day and moment are fixed for this great appearing. It is unalterably fixed. None of God's judgments have been dismissed. They all have an appointment on a certain day and hour. This world has an appointment with God. The "Day of the Lord" has never been adjourned, changed, altered, nor cancelled. "The hour of that event is known to God and to God alone. It is, therefore, clear that speculation regarding the time of the Second Coming is nothing less than blasphemy, for the man who so speculates is seeking to wrest from God secrets which belong to God alone. It is not any man's duty to speculate; it is his duty to prepare himself, and to watch."[2] Acts 1:7, "And He said to them, 'It is not for you to know times or seasons, which the Father has put in His own authority.'"

Second, it is a day of suddenness (vv. 27, 43). 1 Thessalonians 5:3 warns, "For when they say, 'Peace (prosperity) and safety (security),' then sudden (unexpected and unforeseen) destruction comes upon them, as labor pains upon a pregnant woman. And they shall not escape." The following appeared in *Decision Magazine*: "When God was granting children to my wife, Kathy, and me, many expectant parents were attending special classes for childbirth. Natural childbirth was 'in.' Husbands were supposed to learn about the process to learn about the wives, and then assist in the actual delivery. Kathy and I did not attend classes; we figured that we would let the doctors do it all. *Big Mistake*! Our second child could not wait. The time from the first labor pain to crowning – when the baby's head starts to appear – was only about 15 minutes, and our room was at the top of a narrow stairway. We were stuck, and I was not ready. We had alerted our doctor, and he was meeting us at the hospital, but I could not get in touch with him. I had no idea what to do.

Fortunately, our neighbor called the emergency crew, and they were ready. Our daughter arrived safely. But that day, I learned the importance of being ready. I had known that our baby was coming, but I was not ready for her to come so quickly, and the story could have ended in tragedy. The last sermon that Jesus gave before His Passion was about being ready. At the climax of His sermon, as recorded in Mark 13, Jesus said, 'No one knows about that day or hour, not even the angels in heaven, nor the Son, but only the Father. Be on guard! Be alert! You do not know when that time will come.'"[3]

It will be as sudden and awesome as lightning, "For as lightning comes from the east and flashes to the west, so also will the coming of the Son of Man be" (v. 27). Christ compares His coming to a great flash of lightning which explodes in the east, then illuminates the earth and sky as far as the west, implying a worldwide event. His coming will be neither doubtful nor obscure, local or limited, or so gradual that it can scarcely be discerned. As lightning bursts forth out of the darkness of the storm and explodes with the brilliance of its illumination, there will be no mistaking that His return has come. There will be no obscurity about His coming again, for it will happen with radiance, greatness, suddenness, and as startling as the lightning. As lightning strikes terror in the hearts of mankind, so will the Second Coming.

It will be as sudden and unexpected as a thief, "But know this, that if the master of the house had known what hour the thief would come, he would have watched and not allowed his house to be broken into" (v. 43). "But know this" means "pay careful attention to what I am about to say." "If" implies the master of the house did not know. "What hour" means "in which of the four quarters of the night." The Jews divided the night into four "watches." The first watch was evening, from 6 – 9 P.M. The second watch was midnight, from 9 – 12 P. M. The third watch, cockcrowing, was from 12 – 3 A.M. The fourth watch, morning, was from 3 – 6 A.M. If a man knows he is to be robbed at night, and knows the hour in which it will happen, he prepares himself for the burglar when he comes. No burglar forewarns that he is coming. People today have less excuse for carelessness than this "master," who had not been forewarned that a thief was coming. The purpose is to alarm the unwary, and to show the necessity of being cautious. The thief does not announce his coming, but arrives stealthily in the dead of the night when men are least expecting danger. Had they known the hour, they would have watched. Further, a thief comes for a certain purpose. He does not take everything in the house. He only takes the most valuable things, the jewels, gold, silver, and the most expensive apparel. Neither does he come to stay. As soon as he obtains what he is after, he leaves. Therefore, Christ will come as a thief at the Rapture and take His saints only. 1 Thessalonians 5:2, 4, "The day of the Lord so comes as a thief in the night...This day should not overtake you as a thief."[2] 2 Peter 3:10, "But the day of the Lord will come as a thief in the night." Revelation 16:15, "Behold, I am coming as a thief. Blessed is he who watches, and keeps his garments, lest he walk naked and they see his shame." Dr. G. Campbell Morgan said, "I never lay my head on the pillow at night without thinking that before the morning dawns the final morning may have dawned."[4]

It is a time of shock and separation. "Then two men will be in the field: one will be taken and the other left. Two women will be grinding at the mill: one will be taken and the other left" (vv. 40, 41). Two men and two women speak of alike occupations, alike unawareness, and alike relationship, because they were near to each other. Two men and two women working together, but how different are their fates! It will be an occasion of a sure separation from companions. Twice, He states, "...one will be taken and the other left." He distinguishes those who are nearest to Him in this world from those who are far from Him. The true believers, His choice and chosen ones, will be taken to glory… the others left to perish. "Taken" means "to lay hold of." Also, "…to take to oneself, take with, or take along," implying separation from companions. Usually, the word involves taking people, and often involves close personal relationship. Further, "…will be taken" is spoken twice, implying the certainty of this event. The Bible says of Enoch's translation to Heaven, "He was not, for God took (carried away, seized) him" (Genesis 5:24). "Vessels of mercy and prepared for glory, or vessels of wrath prepared for ruin, accordingly it will be with them; the one taken to *meet the Lord and His angels in the air, to be forever with Him and them;* the other left to the devil and his angels…God knows how to separate between the precious and the vile, the gold and dross in the same lump, the wheat and chaff from the same floor."[5] "In the field" and "grinding at the mill" tell us that Christ will come unlooked for, as people are busy at their usual occupations. They will be working together at their ordinary occupations, with nothing outwardly to distinguish one from the other, the godly and the evil mingled together. The Second Coming will be so sudden and discriminatory that persons working together will be separated. The masks of hypocrites will be torn away, while revealing the holiness and devotion of the self-denying Christian. Families will be broken up, friendships dissolved, and life-partnerships will come to an end.

The Scottish minister, Horatio Bonar, on one occasion, sat with a number of fellow ministers. He said to them, "Do you really expect Jesus Christ to come today?" One by one, he went around the circle and put that question to each. One by one, they shook their heads, and said, "No, not today." Then, without comment, he wrote on a piece of paper these words and passed it around, "Therefore you also must be ready; for the Son of Man is coming at an hour you do not expect."[6]

The Actions of Society

It will be a day of seduction and deception. Hebrews 6:2 refers to this day as the day of "eternal judgment," unlooked for by most men. Russell Kirk warned, "A good many people fret themselves over the rather improbable speculation that the earth may be blown asunder by nuclear weapons. The grimmer and more immediate prospect is that men and women may be reduced to a sub-human state through limitless indulgence in their own vices – with ruinous consequences to society."[7]

Christ gave two reasons for the seduction and deception: First, because of a misplaced focus, "For as in the days before the flood, they were eating and drinking, marrying and giving in marriage, until the day that Noah entered the ark" (v.38). Christ here explains the attention they were giving to this life rather than what was coming upon them. "They" speaks of how unified they were in their ungodliness, as they were intoxicated with wickedness. They were doing what was necessary. "Eating and drinking" is necessary for the preservation of man's life. "Marrying and giving in marriage" is necessary for the preservation of mankind. However, they were completely consumed by these things. "Eating" has the thought of gnawing food greedily like an animal. It denotes, not a single act, but habitual…a lifestyle. They were focused on this life and not eternal life. They were like the people of Isaiah's day who seemed to have no other reason to live but to consume as much of this life as possible. "'Come,' one says, 'I will bring wine, and we will fill ourselves with intoxicating drink; tomorrow will be as today, and much more abundant'" (Isaiah 56:12). They were living a reckless and consumed life, pursuing worldly pleasure, while judgment was at the door. In 2 Thessalonians 2:12, Paul speaks of those who "had pleasure in unrighteousness," meaning that they delighted in it, allowing it to consume their life, deadening the thought of eternity. Jesus warned in Luke 21:34, 35, "But take heed to yourselves and be on guard, lest your hearts be overburdened and depressed (weighed down) with giddiness and headache and nausea of self-indulgence, drunkenness, and worldly worries and cares pertaining to this life, and [lest] that day come upon you suddenly like a trap or a noose; for it will come upon all who live upon the face of the earth" (The Amplified Bible).

An English nobleman gave a jester a wand, saying, "Keep this until you find a greater fool than yourself." The jester humorously accepted the wand and displayed it on various occasions as entertainment. One day, the nobleman was dying. He called the jester to his bedside, and said, "I am going on a long journey." "Where to?" asked the jester. "I don't know," he replied. "How long will you be gone?" the jester questioned. "I will be gone forever," said the dying nobleman. "What provisions have you made for the trip?" the jester inquired. The nobleman, shrugging his shoulders, answered, "None at all." "Then," said the jester, "take this." Placing the wand in the nobleman's hands, he added, "It belongs to you!"[8]

Second, a mismanaged life, "And did not know until the flood came and took them all away, so also will the coming of the Son of Man be." They were secure and careless. According to 1 Peter 3:20, they had fair and adequate warning through the preaching of Noah, yet they simply ignored the coming disaster. "And did not know" implies "they believed not," or "they chose not to know." Their misplaced focus of eating and drinking was the cause. They could have known, but they chose not to. Because they were sensual, they lived in a false security. They were so taken up with things present and seen, that they had no time, nor heart, nor interest to consider what they were being warned of. "Until the flood came" means that they refused to believe it, yet they could not prevent it. Just because we ignore the thought of the Second Coming in our minds in no way delays it in the mind of God – "the flood came" – "so also will the coming of the Son of Man be." Neglect and carelessness will be an epidemic of the last days. People will be so engaged with the ordinary busyness of life that they will be unconcerned.

Dio Chrysostom warned, "Like men

with sore eyes, they find the light painful, while the darkness, which permits them to see nothing, is restful and agreeable."[9] Such is the mindset of a lost world at the return of Christ!

✝ The Actions of Believers

Christ gives a double command. He says to "watch therefore," and "Therefore you also be ready" (vv. 42a and 44a). "Therefore" (or because of this) is used as an emphasis towards spiritual things regarding the previous solemn examples. Both commands are strong exhortations. "Watch" means to be on the alert, as a guard or sentinel during the day and during the night, keeping your eyes wide open, actively on guard. It implies not only to agree that He will return, but to desire His return, and to be vigilant, always prepared. We are to watch for the signs of His coming, expecting it to be near. Few exhortations are more frequent and urged that to be watchful. In 1 Thessalonians 5:6, Paul states that to not watch and be ready is compared to a state of sleeping. To watch and be ready is to be awake and prepared. "Accordingly then, let us not sleep as the rest do, but let us keep wide awake (alert, watchful, cautious, and on our guard), and let us be sober (calm, collected, and circumspect)" (Amplified Bible). According to 2 Peter 3:11 and 14, it is not enough to "look" for such things. We must also "give diligence." The Amplified Bible reads, in verse 14, "So, beloved, since you are expecting these things, be eager to be found by Him [at His coming] without spot or blemish and at peace [in serene confidence, free from fears and agitating passions and moral conflicts]."

Christ gives a double warning. He says, "...for you do not know," and "for the Son of Man is coming at an hour when you do not expect Him" (vv. 42b and 44b). We are kept in uncertainty, so that we may, every day, expect Him to come any day.

2 Timothy 4:8, "[As to what remains] henceforth there is laid up for me the [victor's] crown of righteousness [for being right with God and doing right], which the Lord, the righteous Judge, will award to me and recompense me on that [great] day – and not to me only, but also to all those who have loved and yearned for and welcomed His appearing (His return)" (The Amplified Bible). A young mother told her minister, "There must be something wrong with me. You asked us

this morning whether we 'love the Lord's appearing,' and I don't. I'm happy with my family. I guess you could say I'm reconciled to Christ's coming back, but it's not exactly top priority on my lists of wants."[10]

Chapter Three

The Apathy of Those Days

(Matthew 25:1 – 13)

The French-Canadian city of Quebec has an interesting history. Visitors can view the Plains of Abraham where the English forces of General Wolfe won Quebec from the French. When visitors see the steep ascent that Wolfe's men had to make up the face of the great rocky cliffs, they are amazed that they succeeded. A band of boys should have been able to hold off a force of soldiers from scaling such cliffs and gaining the heights. Yet, Wolfe and his men made the ascent and gained the citadel. Why? Because the overconfident defenders became careless and pleasure-loving, and, one night, when they were off guard, the enemy saw his opportunity, scaled the heights, and took the city. Quebec fell because its defenders became apathetical and failed to watch.[1]

Christ begins Matthew chapter 25 with the word "Then." He is referring to "the day" He warned of in chapter 24, giving signs of the times and the end of the age. He spoke of an increase in deception and violence (vv. 5, 6), an acceleration of wars and upheavals, famines, diseases, earthquakes, moral breakdown, betrayal, and hatred (v. 7); sincere love and care fading away (v. 12), the ominous threat of nuclear war (v. 29), the miraculous rebirth of the nation of Israel (v. 32), a world-wide spirit of apathy and carelessness (vv. 37 – 39), and an increase in those who scoff at the thought of the Lord's return (v. 48). Instead of encouraging pessimism, He is giving an admonition: "When you see these things, know that it (His return) is near – at the door!"

Here, in Matthew 25, in His parable of "The Ten Virgins," Christ is telling of the terrible predicament people will find themselves in if they do not stay prepared for His return. The emphasis is "watch" and "be ready." In doing so, He speaks of three things:

First: a wedding, symbolic of His second coming. In Christ's day, normally there were three stages in the matrimonial process. First came the engagement. This was a formal agreement made by the fathers of the bride and the groom. Second: then came the betrothal, where a ceremony was held in the house of the bride's parents. Here mutual promises were made by the contracting parties before witnesses, and the bridegroom gave presents to his wife-to-be. This was a binding ceremony, though the actual marriage had not taken place. It was so legally binding that if the man died during this period of time, the woman was regarded as a widow. Canceling the betrothal was not permitted. If, however, such an action was taken, it was parallel to divorce. Third: after a period of about a year, the marriage took place. The bridegroom, accompanied by his friends, would go to get the bride and bring her back to his father's house where a marriage feast was held. Most likely, it was this procession that the ten virgins in the parable are pictured as going out to meet. Here, though, the bridegroom is not in town, but off at a distance, and the exact hour of his arrival is uncertain.

Second: ten virgins, which speak of the Church. There were ten. "Ten" is the number of completeness in the Bible. A group of people were considered complete when ten were present. An ancient Jewish law said that wherever there were ten Jews, a synagogue could be built. Ten, then, is the number of completeness. Since there were ten virgins, it speaks of the Church. "Virgins" speak of their beauty and purity. They represent the Church, because it is pure and holy. They speak of the professing members of the Church awaiting the return of Christ. This is not a story of service, but one of personal relationship. It is a picture of an individual relation with and attitude towards Christ. Five were "foolish." In verse 2, in the KJV and NKJV and other translations, the "wise" are listed first, but in the original Greek, the "foolish" come first in verse 2, as in verses 3 and 4. Some believe that this means they were a more prominent class than the others were. The Amplified Bible says they were "thoughtless, without forethought." Others translate "foolish" as "stupid!" The five foolish speak of those who are spiritually careless, and who "suppose" they are where they should be with God. However, though of the same profession as others in the Church, their characters were vastly different in the sight of God, proven by the result. Simply put, they were unprepared. Five were "wise." The Amplified Bible says they were

"sensible, intelligent, and prudent."
"'Wise' also means 'to have in mind, be mindful of, to think of.' The wise virgins used their heads! They were thoughtful, foresighted, providing for emergencies – which often happen."[2] Simply put, they were prepared. Their conduct refers to those who are prepared for the coming of Christ. The ten virgins were all "Christian," for they all belonged to the same circle of intimate friends. The fault of the foolish, sadly, was carelessness and negligence, caused by presumption and indifference. The prudence of the wise, in contrast, was their diligence and perseverance to stay prepared.

Third, the bridegroom speaks of Christ, a man newly married. He comes from heaven to take His bride home. He returned at the most unexpected moment, and five of those virgins were "shut out" (left behind). Believers are now engaged and betrothed to Christ, but the finalizing of the marriage is reserved for that great day, when the bride, the Lamb's wife, "...has made herself ready" (Revelation 19:7).

Christ gave seven warnings:

A Wedding Promised

(v. 10)

"The bridegroom came" (v. 10b). There will be a wedding – Christ will return! The second coming of Christ is dealt with 1,845 times in the Bible, 318 of which are found in the New Testament. Seven out of ten chapters in the New Testament refer to His return. For every one time in the Bible the first coming is mentioned, the second coming is mentioned eight times. Christ referred to His return 21 times, and over 50 times men are exhorted to be ready for the return of Jesus Christ.

In John 14:3, Jesus declared, "I will come again." This statement is in the present tense in the Greek. It is not a future statement. So, why is it spoken in the present tense? When the Greeks wanted to say something that could never be refuted, and so positive that they said it as though it was happening, or had already happened. They used present or past tense to verify future absolutes. Christ is saying, "I'm as good as here. That's how secure My promise is!"

John Wesley White, in his book *Re-entry*, wrote, "Alexander Maclaren aptly noted, 'The primitive Church thought more about the second coming of Jesus Christ than about death or even heaven.

They were not looking for a cleft in the ground called a grave, but for a cleavage in the sky call Glory. They were not watching for the 'undertaker,' but for the 'Uppertaker.' They felt that man's chief end was to get right with God, or to be left when Christ returned. Winston Churchill's favorite American song was, 'Mine eyes have seen the glory of the coming of the Lord!' That was the vision of the ancient apostles, one which gave them dynamism and direction."[3]

Self-Deception

(vv. 10 – 12)

Not everyone who thinks he/she is ready when He comes is really ready. There was a shut door, "…and the door was shut" (v. 10d). The last time we hear of the foolish, they are all outside! They never took God seriously.

There was a desperate plea, "Afterward the other virgins came also, saying, 'Lord, Lord, open to us!'" (v. 11) They were too late to do what they should have done, too late for the bridal procession and festival. Their desperate cry was not answered as they had expected. It is too late to ask for mercy when the day of grace has ceased. Isaiah 55:6 calls all men to, "Seek the Lord while He may be found, call upon Him while He is near." There will be a day when He will not be found to listen. They should have said, "Lord, Lord," while it was the opportune time, because Christ promised, "Knock and it will be opened to you" (Matthew 7:7). Now, it was too late.

In an article called, "When Christ Returns – Will You Be Ready?" John D.

Harvey wrote, "'Where will we *ever* find someone to fit that tuxedo?' I asked. What had seemed like an endless wait the previous night had suddenly become a frantic scramble of last-minute preparations. My wife-to-be, Anita Burns, and I had been mildly concerned at the wedding rehearsal when one of my groomsmen had failed to arrive. The next morning, on our wedding day, our attitude changed drastically when we received word that he was not coming at all. Should we proceed with the people on hand, or should we try to find a substitute groomsman? Fortunately, one of my bride's former professors fit all the measurements of the rented tuxedo – if he held his stomach in! The wedding went ahead as planned, but I could certainly identify with the panic of the five young women who tried to make last-minute preparations in Jesus' parable traditionally known as 'The Parable of the Ten Virgins.'"[4]

There was an absolute denial, "But he answered, and said, 'Assuredly, I say to you, I do not know you'" (v. 12). "I do not know you" means "I do not recognize your right to enter." It is often used in the sense of approving, loving, and recognizing as true friends. Having missed the bridal procession and the festival, the bridegroom could only respond from within that he had no knowledge of them. Psalm 95:10, 11, "It is a people who go astray in their hearts, and they do not know My ways. So I swore in My wrath, 'They shall not enter My rest.'"

Carelessness Verses Preparation

(vv. 1, 2 – 4)

They were religiously minded, "The kingdom of heaven shall be likened to ten virgins who took their lamps and went out to meet the bridegroom" (v. 1). This speaks of expecting His return. All ten virgins had a common expectation. They all were waiting for someone. All ten represent those who believe that the end of the age will come just as Christ describes it. Believers are to not only believe and look for, but to love and desire Christ to come. They are to conduct themselves, also, with regard to it.

There was foresight... and no sight (vv. 2 – 4). The difference in the two classes was the foresight of the one and the negligence of the other. Five had foresight and five had no sight, "Now five of them were wise, and five were foolish" (v. 2). The Bible divided them into two groups: Five were wise and five were foolish. They were all alike in their response to meet the bridegroom, "Then all the virgins arose" (v. 7), and they all had the same type lamps. Yet, they differed deeply. They were all alike in their knowledge of the bridegroom, all had lamps, all slept, and all arose to meet the cry, "Behold, the bridegroom is coming" (v. 6). But it was at this point that the difference between the virgins was revealed. The foolish failed to keep themselves prepared. The wise knew what to expect and prepared for it. The foolish were guilty of careless presumption…presuming they had enough oil. "Those who were foolish took their lamps and took no oil with them" (v. 3). "Lamps" is best read as "torches." They were supported on poles, and filled with rags that required a regular soaking with oil. If a torch was to stay burning, it was necessary to have a supply of oil adequate enough to keep the rags burning. The foolish five evidently had soaked their rags in oil when they departed, but took nothing extra. "Lamps" speak of our life, that which is outward. It is how we live before men. "Oil" refers to our relationship with God, due to the indwelling Holy Spirit. It speaks of that which is inward. Outwardly, there was no observable difference between the foolish and the wise. But the foolish took no oil with them. They only had the lamp of profession, and a nominal, head-belief... obviously religiously active, with not one spark of divine life. It was not that the foolish virgins did

not have any oil at all; they had some...
but not enough. The oil reservoirs were
small, so the wise and diligent would
carry another container from which to
refill them. This the foolish failed to do.
While the wise maintained the grace of
God by continual recourse to God, the
foolish were satisfied with their spiritual
condition. They made no effort to keep
their spiritual life healthy and active by
the renewal of the Holy Spirit. They were
guilty of supposing they had enough oil
to last until the bridegroom came. They
had just enough oil to burn their lamps
for a while, to make a show with, giving
the impression that they intended to meet
the bridegroom. They had a lamp of
profession in their hands, but not in their
hearts. Theirs was an outward show, a
form of faith, while neglecting the true
inward life of spiritual health. They had

71

no reality, while having the appearance that they did. They were motivated by religious ways, but were lacking in spiritual life. They may have impressed others, but were not approved of by Christ. The parents of Jesus supposed that He was with them, and journeyed on without Him (Luke 2:41 – 46). It is possible to suppose our life is pleasing to God, making us guilty of spiritual presumption. They delighted in their profession, and trusted in it as if they had all that was needed for their spiritual life. They were void of the "renewing of the Holy Spirit" (Titus 3:5). Too many people try to live on some wonderful experience of the past, forgetting that we need a daily supply of the Spirit, His Word, and fellowship with Christ in prayer.

The wise were diligent, "But the wise

took oil in their vessels with their lamps"
(v. 4). These virgins soaked their rags
with oil, but also took an extra supply of
oil for emergencies. They knew that the
time of the bridegroom's coming was
uncertain, so they furnished
themselves with oil. They had a healthy
condition within, verifying their
profession. While looking for His
immediate return, they also prepared for
a long wait... and to prepare for the
worst. They knew that there is the need
of daily preparation and constant
watchfulness for His coming. They did
not trust in a past experience, however
overwhelming. They are constantly
reaching forth to what is ahead, in prayer,
self-denial, and faithfulness.

A Sudden Event

(vv. 5, 6)

It happened when they all slumbered and slept, "But while the bridegroom was delayed, they all slumbered and slept" (v. 5). The bridegroom "delayed." The end was not yet. However, as the time of waiting grew long (longer than they thought), the first excitement faded, some left their first love and it was growing cold. Then... "they all slumbered and slept." This means "to become drowsy and nod." "Slumbered" implies the nodding and napping of those who sit up at night. "Slept" means they began to sleep. They all began to nod, and were sleeping, so it was not sinful, only natural. Both groups ceased for a while to think of the coming of the bridegroom. However, the wise could afford to sleep because they were ready.

It implies that those who are ready need not live in tension and stress, but in peace and calmness of soul. The life that is truly consecrated and committed to God is a life in which there is inner peace, poise, and strength, free from worry. There is a difference between the slumber of the wise and the deep sleep of the foolish. The wise have a sleep with their sense of hearing on the alert, and listening for the sound of their redemption. However busy and occupied they become, it never is allowed to affect their "spiritual ears." They are the ones who have no care, no eyes, and no thought for anything except Christ and His hour of return. They "wait for His Son from heaven" (1 Thessalonians 1:10). It was ridiculous, though, for the foolish to sleep, for they were unprepared. The bridegroom "delayed," that is, he did not come as soon as expected. Time revealed their shallowness. Note that they "slumbered," and then they "slept." Knox has, "…grew drowsy and fell asleep." It speaks of not looking for His return, due to being overly consumed with the world's business and amusements, thinking very little of eternity. One degree of carelessness leads to another. Those who allow themselves to slumber will soon be sleeping. This speaks of the slow but sure process of spiritual decay. They were not openly wicked and disobedient, and that is what gives this parable such a shocking meaning. It is not enough to have been awakened. There must be a constant perseverance of watchfulness. To neglect is to treat our Bridegroom with contempt. Neglect here is damnable. We have here the very spirit of procrastination.

It happened at midnight, "And at midnight a cry was heard, 'Behold, the bridegroom is coming; go out to meet him!'" (v. 6) Actually this reads, "Look! The bridegroom!" "A cry was heard" emphasizes the suddenness of the event. In the Book of Revelation, six times Christ says, "Behold, I come quickly." No one knows when the second interruption of the world's plans will happen. It is the baseless conclusion that the Lord will not come quickly that deceives men into carelessness. It came suddenly, in the dead of the night. "Midnight" is when deep sleep comes upon people, and to be awakened is irritating. This speaks of how unexpected His return will be. The time of the redeemed is fixed, and it will come.

Though He tarry, He will come at last. His first coming, which was long waited for, did not happen until the "fullness of time" had come. Likewise, His second coming, though long delayed, is not forgotten. He will come at "midnight," when it is least expected. He is coming to reward, judge, and punish. It was at midnight that the firstborn of Egypt died, and God's people were delivered (Exodus 12:29). Death came to the foolish rich man at "night," when it was least expected (Luke 12:20). Christ will come when the Father decides… to show that He is sovereign over man and his plans. "A cry was heard." When Christ comes, He will descend "with a shout" (1 Thessalonians 4:16). "Go out to meet him" is the call to those who are watching and are prepared.

Lack

(vv. 7 – 10,11)

The horror of self-deception will grip the soul, due to "lack." There was the lack of personal relationship, "Then all those virgins arose and trimmed their lamps. And the foolish said to the wise, 'Give us some of your oil, for our lamps are going out'" (v. 7). "Trimmed" means, "To put in order," i.e., cleaned the wicks, lighted them, and adjusted the flames. To trim a lamp was to remove the burned out wick that hinders the light. It signifies the removing of anything that keeps us from being our best for God. It means to shake off the sloth and slumber of worldly ease and carnal distractions, to keep the affections of our heart in focus. The Amplified Bible has, "Then all those virgins got up and put their own lamps in order." They had all made some progress, more or less, in the way of godliness. They all did what was needed to put themselves in position to receive the bridegroom. However, the foolish had trusted in their own goodness, convincing themselves that they were ready.

The foolish had been self-deceived, but now saw their true condition, "And the foolish said to the wise, 'Give us some of your oil, for our lamps are going out'" (v. 8). When they were awakened, there was no time for them to do anything except to re-fuel their lamps. Their lamps were going out; there was still a small, weak flame, but it was dying, and almost gone. They got their wicks ready to light. Suddenly, they realized they had no oil in their lamps, because they had brought no further supply with them.

"Going out" is the same word as "quench," where we are admonished to, "Quench not the Spirit," in 1 Thessalonians 5:19. "Quench" means "to suppress or subdue." This proves that their lamps had once been lighted. Had they not been previously lighted, they could not go out. Some make conversion everything, edification nothing. They seldom have a serious thought about and earnest effort to maintain within themselves their spiritual life. If we do not renew our supply of grace, the flame will burn low. Their false hope and confidence was fading. They appealed to their prudent companions to help them. As they began to make ready, they became alarmed, anxious, and fearful. When they appeal for assistance, they discover it is too late. We cannot borrow that which must be personally obtained from earnest prayer and diligent seeking of God. The merits of others will not compensate for our lack. There is no such thing as second-hand faith. A man may teach others about God, admonish towards Christ, and set a godly example, but he cannot give us oil – faith, life, etc. External religion will carry a man so far in this world, but it will not take him to the other world. Their concern was too late, because they saw no need for diligence while waiting. If they would have asked God for oil, He would have given it to them, but there is no buying when the market is closed. This is a warning against neglect concerning the matters of the soul, or trusting in last-minute repentance.

There was a lack of foresight and diligence. "But the wise answered, saying, 'No, lest there should not be enough for us and you; but go rather to those who sell, and buy for yourselves'" (v. 9). Some read this as more stern and pointed, "Never! There will certainly not be enough for us and you!" They could not render last-minute assistance to them. It was now midnight, merchants were closed, so the purchase could not be made in time. Lost opportunities never return! There are some things which cannot be obtained at the last moment. It is far too late for a student to start preparing when the day of the examination has come. They were told, "Go buy for yourselves." The lesson is that saving grace is a personal possession and cannot be transferred. On that day, no one can deliver his brother. Each one is, in this respect, responsible for his own destiny. Our spiritual life is not dependent on someone else. Everyone must take care of himself. We must have God's grace as our own. We will be judged individually, entirely on our own. Spiritual life and power can only be imparted by God to those who have fulfilled His requirements. They were refused by the wise, and soon were to be rejected of God. The foolish virgins found that it was impossible to borrow oil when they discovered they needed it. No one can borrow a relationship with God; he must possess it for himself. Those who would reign with Christ must have grace of their own. The fellowship and communion of the saints is needful and beneficial, yet a personal relationship with Christ is necessary for salvation. Everyone must give an account of himself.

There was a lack of concern, "And when they went to buy... those who were ready went in to him to the wedding" (v. 10a, c). The foolish put off what was needed until the last moment, and they did not have time to do it then. They did take the advice of the wise, though, but they had not taken advantage of the opportunity beforehand. When it was easier to prepare, they had been careless. In Luke 21:34, Jesus warned of a life-style that would cause the day of His return to catch some "unexpectedly." The wise went immediately into the wedding. They went into the wedding, because they had readied themselves for it ahead of time. Not only did they meet the bridegroom, but accompanied him into the joyful bridal feast.

There was a belated desperation, "Afterward, the other virgins came also, saying, 'Lord, Lord open to us!'" (v. 11) "Lord, Lord" means that they claimed a relationship. By repeating, "Lord" twice shows their earnestness in seeking admission. It is a cry of desperation, pleading, and demanding. Such is the condition of the foolish who expect to go to heaven, but will be shut out. Multitudes will seek entrance into heaven when it is too late.

The Cost

(v. 10)

"And the door was shut" (v. 10d). It was customary to shut the doors when all guests were assembled. The door was shut for the security of those inside, and for the exclusion of those on the outside. In this parable, when the door was shut, there was no more entrance for any one. Those who have been watchful and diligent will accompany Christ to heaven. Those who have been neglectful, careless, and presumptuous, having not made their calling and election sure, will be shut out. The door is open now, but the time is coming when it must be shut. This is perpetual exclusion from the presence of God in outer darkness. Christ made it very clear concerning the man in Hades, "And besides all this, between us and you a great chasm has been fixed, in order that those who want to pass from this [place] to you may not be able, and no one may pass from there to us" (Luke 16:26) (The Amplified Bible). One other time the door was shut. Genesis 7:13 – 16, "Noah and Noah's sons…and Noah's wife and the three wives of his sons with them, entered the ark – they and every beast after its kind…And they went into the ark…So those that entered…went in as God had commanded him; and, the Lord shut the door."

Warning

(v. 13)

"Watch therefore, for you know neither the day nor the hour in which the Son of Man is coming." Revelation 16:15, "Behold, I come as a thief; blessed is he that watches." "Watches" means "to stay awake, alert, and vigilant," i.e., keep your eyes wide open! Previously, Christ had said, "Watch therefore, for you do not know what hour your Lord is coming" (Matthew 24:42). It is repeated here as a double caution and warning. Christ is warning us all to keep our hearts with the utmost diligence and care, remaining awake and watching. The time of His return is unknown, therefore every day and every hour we must be ready, refusing to slumber and sleep.

Chapter Four

The Apostasy of Those Days

(Romans 1:18 – 32)

Billy Graham, in a message, "You Can Know the Truth," expressed, "I read an article about the great Beijing-to-Paris car race that was first run in 1907. Today, it's still one of the longest and most grueling automobile races in the world. The route covers 16,000 kilometers across two continents, eleven countries, three deserts, and too many rivers to count. When the race was first run, finding the way was the major problem. Today, each car is equipped with a global positioning system, an electronic device that sends a signal to a satellite. It shows the driver and the navigator their position on a computerized map. But even with this high-tech navigational help, the basic challenge of the race remains the same. One navigator said, 'We'll always know where we are, but the problem is where *should* we be?' That seems to summarize a great deal of the tension in our world today. In our countries, in our homes, in our families, and deep within our hearts we may know where we are. The problem is where *should* we be? Truth is important in navigation. It is important in mathematics, and it is important in chemistry. But truth is *absolutely essential* in the spiritual realm."[1]

The Psalmist wrote, "If we have forgotten the name of our God, or stretched out our hands to a foreign god, would not God search this out? For He knows the secrets of the heart" (Psalm 44:20, 21). "This is the first step in apostasy; men first forget the true, and then adore the false."[2]

In Romans 1:18 – 32, we are given a process of degeneration of the days of Noah, being duplicated in this modern era. It is the most graphic language of the Bible, describing how a society drifts from the truth of God to one of reprobate minds, in fifteen short verses. Remember, "But as the days of Noah were, so also will the coming of the Son of Man be" (Matthew 24:37).

We are given three descriptions:

The Revelation of God
The Rebellion of Man
The Release of God

The Revelation of God

(vv. 18 – 20)

God has revealed His attitude towards sin, "For the wrath of God is revealed from heaven against all ungodliness and unrighteousness of men, who suppress the truth in unrighteousness" (v. 18). "Wrath" speaks of His personal feeling and attitude towards sin. It describes how God hates sin. It does not speak of His punishment of sin, but His personal emotion towards all sin. When we describe a person as "ungodly," we tend to think of one who is immoral or extremely wicked. *However, "ungodly" simply means "ungodlike," in heart and life, while, at the same time being considered a respectful citizen of society.* He is one who shows little or no reverence towards God's Person.* Actually, the word

92

"expresses the insult and blasphemy involved in sin. There are multitudes of thousands who live lives that are circumspect and socially acceptable, but are nevertheless 'ungodly,' or 'godless,' because they pay no attention to God. A lack of reverence for God and sacred things – for instance, the time and place of worship – is what constitutes real ungodliness. A generation that desecrates the Lord's Day, and lives without any reference to God, is guilty of the sin of 'ungodliness.' Against such an attitude of indifference to the divine, God's wrath is revealed."[3] This is followed by "unrighteousness," which is a wrong attitude inwardly, and a lack of a right conduct outwardly.

During the first World War, a luxurious French villa lay in the path of the advancing armies. Although deserted, it was shelled and left with large holes in its stone sides. A few swine, which had somehow avoided being killed, rooted their way into the magnificent and beautiful drawing room. Over the expensive, velvet carpet, the pigs tracked their muddy feet, overturned the upholstered furniture, tore the expensive draperies, and chewed anything they thought would satisfy their hunger. The beauty, the elegance, the cultural characteristics of the place meant nothing to their animal nature. They were not the intellectual or spiritual qualities of the owner. To the "ungodly" and "unrighteous," the glories of knowing God is like the French villa was to the swine. *Not being partakers of the Divine nature, they have no desire for what is godly and righteous.[4]

God has revealed His personal existence in man's conscience and in creation (vv. 19, 20). He has given His personal revelation in man's conscience, "Because what may be known of God is manifest in them, for God has shown it to them" (v. 19). The universal objective knowledge of God as Creator is in all men. Paul says it, "...is manifest in them," meaning the knowledge of God is apparent and evident in their heart and conscience. He has, "...shown it to them," through their intellect and creation. Hebrews 8:10 says that God has written His laws in human minds and hearts. Hebrews 9:14 declares men have a conscience meant to govern their lives in the knowledge, will, and purposes of God.

President George Washington said, *"Labor to keep alive in your breast that little spark of celestial called conscience."[5] "The Greek word for conscience means, '...a knowing with, i.e., a co-knowledge [with oneself], the witness born to your conduct by conscience, that faculty by which you apprehend the will of God, the sense of guiltiness before God, and the process of thought which considers good or bad. Constitutional scholar, Robert Bork, was asked, 'What is wrong with the world?' He answered, "We have lost our common denominator of moral language."[6]

Further, God has revealed Himself in creation, "For since the creation of the world, His invisible attributes are clearly seen, being understood by the things that are made, even His eternal power and Godhead, so that they are without excuse" (v. 20). The invisible things of God, His power, deity, might, etc., can be seen in nature. All a man has to do is accept the law of cause and effect, which says that every cause must have an adequate effect. This "massive" universe demands that Someone of unlimited power and wisdom had to have created it. Such is so obvious, that man is "without excuse," i.e., without any defense. The Amplified Bible states, "For ever since the creation of the world His invisible nature and attributes, that is, His eternal power and divinity, have been made intelligible and clearly discernable in and through the things that have been made (His handiworks). So [men] are without excuse [altogether without any defense or justification]." "Nature is God's greatest evangelist" (Jonathan Edwards).[7]

In Psalm 101:3, we read, "I hate the work of them who turn aside." "Turn aside" is used of an unruly horse, refusing to be restrained. It also applies to a rebellious man, who is headstrong, ungovernable in his passions and the gratification of them, and completely irreverent towards God and His will. This leads us to the second step of the process of degeneration.

The Rebellion of Man

(vv. 21 – 23, 25)

"The late Joseph Parker preached a powerful sermon on 'The Stupidity of the Specialist.' His text was, 'The stone which the builders rejected, the same is the head of the corner' (Luke 20:17). Mind you, the stone that *the builders* – the experts, the specialists, of all people – rejected! Our civilization is crumbling, because the experts have rejected the only foundation that will endure."[8]

In his rebellion, man took four downward steps:

First, he chose to turn from God, "Because, although they knew God, they did not glorify Him as God, nor were thankful, but became futile in their thoughts, and their foolish hearts were darkened" (v. 21). <u>"Hearts" speak of the way they thought and reasoned in their minds.</u> Paul says it can become "darkened," i.e., lose its ability to see evil as evil and sin as sin. Christ warned, "Your eye is the lamp of your body; when your eye (your conscience) is sound and fulfilling its office, your whole body is full of light; but when it is not sound and is not fulfilling its office, your body is full of darkness. Be careful, therefore, that the light that is in you is not darkness" (Luke 11:34, 35 - The

Amplified Bible). Though they had knowledge of Him, they, being unthankful for the revelation given them, turned their backs on God. They became completely self-centered, lovers of themselves. Everything man tried to satisfy himself ended in futility. His thoughts and hearts were darkened, as he developed his own idea of right and wrong. He eliminated God as his moral compass. The Amplified Bible states, "They became futile and godless in their thinking [with vain imaginings, foolish reasoning, and stupid speculations], and their senseless minds were darkened." The Psalmist said, "Israel would have none of Me" (Psalm 81:11). They were not content with God alone. He was not good enough for them, so their hearts went from Him to other things.

Second, this led to self-deception, "Professing to be wise, they became fools" (v. 22). Believing that he had achieved mental excellence in its highest and fullest sense, he was actually a very foolish and stupid person. Now, nothing is black or white. Everything is a shade of grey, because of a twisted and perverted mind. "The easiest thing of all is to deceive one's self; for what a man wishes he generally believes to be true" (Demosthenes).[9]

Third, he became his own god, "And changed the glory of the incorruptible God into an image made like corruptible man – and birds and four-footed beasts and creeping things" (v. 23). He changed ("to exchange one thing for another)" the truth of God, dethroning God, and enthroning himself. They reduced God to the image of a man, and refused to glorify Him as God. This led to everything, and all things, as objects of worship. According to Genesis 3:5, the first lie of the Bible is Satan's assertion to Eve, "You can be like God." When man becomes his own god, he dethrones Jehovah God from his heart and enthrones Satan as his god, whether he is aware of it or not. This is what the humanists are guilty of today. The result has been abortion, euthanasia, acceptance of deviant lifestyles, etc. Man has normalized the abnormal, making himself the standard for conduct, while calling it "progress."

Amos D. Millard, D. Min., wrote, "Humanism is a system of thought and action which holds that man is capable of self-fulfillment, peace on earth, and right ethical conduct without recourse to God. It is thus a religion which deifies man and dethrones God."[10] A good illustration of this is seen in a very popular TV show of times past: "An army doctor is against war. He is against bigotry. He is compassionate. He loves children. He will deny himself and work long hours to save life. He is a good guy. He does what Christians ought to do. Yet, this same doctor is profane and vulgar. He sleeps with any willing nurse. He is a man of the world, and is totally irreligious. The whole thrust of the show is that the man is within his rights when he lives as he pleases. What he does is his own affair. *He doesn't have to feel guilty, because he has not violated his own idea of correct behavior.* The inference is that there is not a higher authority to whom he has to give an account for his actions."[11]

Fourth, he embraced "the lie," "Who

exchanged the truth of God for the lie, and worshipped and served the creature rather than the Creator, who is blessed forever. Amen" (v. 25). The root cause of this is found in verse 18b, "Who suppress the truth in unrighteousness." Man "held down, or repressed," his revelation of God. God made Himself known, yet man refused to acknowledge and submit to the truth given him. Again, "exchanged" means to "exchange one thing for another." The end result is that he believes "the lie." Man so turned from God, that he cast God aside, and worshipped creation (himself).

According to 2 Thessalonians 2:10b – 12, because people do not welcome and love God's truth, He will send them a "strong delusion," allowing them to further wander and stray away from Him, releasing them to their own deceit. They will answer to Him on judgment day, "Because they did not welcome the Truth, but refused to love it that they might be saved. Therefore God sends upon them a misleading influence, a working of error and a strong delusion, to make them believe what is false, in order that all may be judged and condemned who did not believe in [who refused to adhere to, trust in, and rely on] the Truth, but [instead] took pleasure in unrighteousness" (The Amplified Bible). This leads to the final process of degeneration.

The Release of God

(vv. 24, 26 – 32)

Three times in these verses, we read "God gave them up." "The verb is *paradidomi,* which means 'to give or hand over,' 'give or deliver up,' as to prison or judgment. Here it clearly refers to a judicial punishment for man's willful, deliberate rejection of God. To have God "let one go" is the worst fate that can overtake any human being. Yet, that is the inevitable result of stubborn refusal to let God have His way. A. T. Robertson writes, 'The words sound to us like clods on the coffin as God leaves men to work their own wicked will.'"[12] He handed them over to themselves! Like a rebellious child who is determined to not be under any restraint, so God released them to their own self-determination and self-destruction. He withdrew His restraint and the carnal nature took control. God would not violate man's free will to force him to do something he had no desire for. They persisted, so He allowed them

106

complete freedom to follow their depraved natures. The result was the most vile and unthinkable immorality. This great "give up of God" was (and is) to:

First, uncleanness and lusts, "Therefore God also gave them up to uncleanness, in the lusts of their hearts, to dishonor their bodies among themselves" (v. 24). They became driven and consumed with a spirit of uncleanness and lust of every kind. Leaving all restraint, they were impure in their own hearts which led to sexual impurity. "Abandoning themselves to the degrading power of sin" (Amplified Bible), they were driven by a passionate craving to do that which is dishonorable.

In Ephesians 4:19, Paul describes them, "In their spiritual apathy, they have become callous and past feeling and reckless, and have abandoned themselves [a prey] to unbridled sensuality, eager and greedy to indulge in every form of impurity [that their depraved desires may suggest and demand]" (The Amplified Bible). "'Unbridled sensuality' is from the word 'lasciviousness,' meaning 'lacking in moral discipline, having no regard for accepted moral standards. The word comes from the Latin word 'lascivia,' meaning loose, runaway passion and lust. It signifies licentiousness, lawlessness…the casting off of all restraints. It also represents all that's filthy, degrading, lewd, and obscene."[13]. Christ called this "unbridled sensuality" as a sin of the heart in Mark 7:20 – 22. Russell Kirk warned, "A good many people fret themselves over the rather improbable speculation that the earth may be blown asunder by nuclear weapons. The grimmer and more immediate prospect is that men and women may be reduced to a sub-human state through limitless indulgence in their own vices – with ruinous consequences to society."[14]

Second, vile passions (vv. 26, 27): They entered into that which is sexually disgraceful, "For this reason God gave them up to vile passions. For even their women exchanged the natural use for what is against nature" (v. 26). "Vile" means that which is dishonorable and degrading. They became inflamed with a lust that could not be satisfied, "Likewise also the men, leaving the natural use of the woman, burned in their lust for one another, men with men committing what is shameful, and receiving in themselves the penalty of their error which was due" (v. 27). Being controlled by depraved desires, they committed all types of immodesty, and did that which will (and did) bring God's judgment (Genesis 6:11). "In a major denominational magazine, the pastor of a homosexual congregation stated, 'I'm a gay man, and a minister. I expect to go home tonight to my gay lover with whom I have lived for thirteen years. Tomorrow, I expect to preach to my congregation and to administer communion to them. And I thank God that I feel good about it all.'"[15] Such a mindset leads us to the final "give up of God."

Third, a reprobate mind (vv. 28 – 32): "And even as they did not like to retain God in their knowledge, God gave them over to a debased mind, to do those things which are not fitting" (v. 28). The Amplified Bible states, "And so, since they did not see fit to acknowledge God or approve of Him, or consider Him worth the knowing, God gave them over to a base and condemned mind to do things not proper or decent but loathsome." Man reached a place where he despised everything that restrained him. Not that he tried to remove the thought of God from his mind, but he just would not allow God to be his absolute truth. "A debased mind" is one that is void of judgment. It is a mind that cannot distinguish between good and evil, thus establishes its own concept of right and wrong.

They rejected God, so He rejected them. In verses 29 – 32 is the result of man being filled with sin. Listed are twenty-one frightful sins… sins of thought, word, and deed. They are against both one's self and against one's neighbor. Verse 32 tells us that man reaches such a place of moral bondage and depravity that, though he knows what he is doing will bring the judgment of God, he does it anyway, even applauding those that live such a lifestyle. It is a unity of evil, "Who, knowing the righteous judgment of God, that those who practice such things are worthy of death, not only do the same, but also approve of those who practice them."

The Road to Apostasy

1. A rejection of Biblical authority. There are no concrete absolutes. My ideas are equal to yours.

2. Neutrality. Whatever is said, believed, and practiced is acceptable.

3. Compromise. Any and all thought, lifestyles, etc., is allowed for the sake of unity.

4. Anything less is considered intolerance or bigotry.

5. Apostasy. Anything is condoned, nothing absolute is believed, and the truth of God is mocked and ridiculed.

When the doctrinal absolutes of God are minimized and rejected, men lose the fear of God. Then, there are no restraints. The only alternative is the rejection and give up of God. Banquets in ancient times were usually held at night in brilliantly lit rooms, and anybody who was excluded from the feast was said to be cast out of the lighted room into the "outer darkness" of the night. In Matthew 8:12, Jesus used such exclusion to liken it to the day of judgment. The expression *outer darkness* takes on greater significance when it is realized what a dread the people of New Testament times had for the darkness. A lamp was usually kept burning all night. To sleep in the dark, as we do today, would be a terrible experience for them. Because of this fear, Jesus could have chosen no better comparison than "outer darkness" to represent the future punishment of the unrighteous.[16]

Chapter Five

The Arranging for Those Days

(Hebrews 11:7)

Martin Luther said, "Live as if Christ died yesterday, rose this morning, and is coming back tomorrow."[1] A traveler chanced upon a beautiful villa situated on the shores of a tranquil lake in Switzerland far from the beaten path of tourists. The traveler knocked at the garden gate, and an aged warden undid its heavy fastenings and welcomed him in. The aged man seemed glad to see him, and showed him around the magnificent garden. "How long have you been here?" the traveler asked. "Twenty-four years." "And how often has your master been here meanwhile?" "Four times." "When was he last here?" "Twelve years ago." "He writes often?" "Never once." "From whom do you receive your pay?" "His agent in Mainland." "But he comes here often?" "He has never been here." "Who does come, then?" "I am almost always alone – it is very, very seldom that even a stranger comes." "Yet you have the garden in such perfect order, everything flourishing, as if you were expecting your master's coming tomorrow!" *"As if he were coming today sir, today,"* exclaimed the old man.[2]

We know nothing of Noah's early life. He first appears in Genesis 5:32. He was the grandson of Methuselah and the great-grandson of Enoch. Most likely, his father, Lamech, was a God-fearing

116

man, and gave his son a proper name meaning "rest," seeing in him something unique for the times. We do know that he lived in a time when the world was universally wicked – violence, moral collapse, godlessness - so much that God said He would destroy the human race (Genesis 6:1 – 7). Noah, however, walked with God, when to do so was not popular. God gave him exact instructions for building the ark (Genesis 6:14 – 16). While engaging in the enormous task of building the ark, he warned men of the coming judgment, as "a preacher of righteousness" (2 Peter 2:5), while God patiently waited for men to repent (1 Peter 3:20). His three sons, Shem, Ham, and Japheth, were born when he was 500 years old (Genesis 5:32). A week before the Flood, God directed Noah and his family into the ark, and supernaturally

117

directed the animals, "...went into the ark to Noah, two by two, of all flesh in which is the breath of life" (Genesis 7:15). When all were safely inside, God shut the door (Genesis 7:16). Following the Flood, Noah built the first recorded altar (Genesis 8:20), and was honored by God with the everlasting covenant of the rainbow, a sign of God's grace and mercy (Genesis 9:12 – 17).

While his society was facing certain judgment and annihilation, Noah "found grace in the eyes of the Lord" (Genesis 6:8). How did he do it? What distinguished him from the others? How was he able to get himself, his wife, his three sons and their wives, into the ark? The answer is found in Hebrews 11:7, "By faith, Noah, being divinely warned of things not yet seen, moved with godly fear, prepared an ark for the saving of his household, by which he condemned the world and became heir of the righteousness which is according to faith.", The Scriptures reveal six things about him.

Intimacy with God

He was a man of intimacy with God, "By faith, Noah, being divinely warned." A parishioner approached his pastor. He said, "Pastor, I have sought a deeper and more meaningful experience with God for a long time now, and yet, I still do not have it. I have read books and articles. I have attempted to obey all the rules, but I am nowhere yet. Does God have favorites?" "No," answered the pastor, God does not have favorites. But He does have intimates."[3]

He was intimate with God because his faith was grounded first on God's Word.

To be "divinely warned" means to be "divinely intimate, something useful, wealth, demand, requirement, and needful."[4] Noah recognized that he must do whatever necessary to be useful to God and to obey His demands. This is what was needed if he was to have a rich relationship with God. In Luke 12:16 - 21, Christ spoke of a very wealthy man who lived completely for worldly gain, but lost his soul. God never condemned the man for his riches, but did warn that while he attained unlimited possessions, he was "not rich [in his relation] to God." The Savior said the man was a "fool!"

Four times in the Genesis account we read, "God said to Noah." This means that God communed with Noah, and declared to him His will and purpose. His faith rested on Divine communication. He had nothing else on which to ground

120

his faith except what God spoke to him. His faith remained strong and resolute throughout the long and severe trials. God had spoken to him, and that was enough. Proverbs 3:32 says, "His secret counsel is with the upright." "Secret" is defined as "to sit down together, consult, take counsel, instruct, a company of persons in close deliberation, intimacy, secret counsel."[5]

John Wanamaker, American Merchant and U. S. Postmaster General from 1889 – 1893, cried, "Oh, Lord, Thou hast told us how to pray. Help us shut the door, shutting out the world and the enemy, and any fever of doubt that spoils prayer. May there be no distinction between our souls and Thee."[6] Abraham walked and worshipped alone, and was given miraculous promises of God. In the solitude of Bethel, Jacob was granted visions of God. When Moses was alone and silent in the desert, he received his divine commission. Joshua, facing the formidable Jericho, as he walked alone, the "Commander of the Army of the Lord" strengthened him. Elisha was alone, plowing his field, when God's purpose was revealed. When Isaiah was in the solitary place of the temple, a live coal touched his lips, and he was sent forth to prophesy. Mary was alone when Gabriel brought her God's purpose for redemption through the miraculous birth of the Messiah.

In the Messianic Psalm 16, verse 8, David said of himself, yet also prophesied of Christ, stating, "I have set the Lord always before me." The literal meaning is, "I was always in His presence, beholding His face."[7] Dr. Henry A. Ironside, as a young preacher visiting the aged Alexander Fraser, was enthralled as one truth after another came from his lips. He fervently asked, "Where did you learn these things?" "On my knees on the mud floor of a little sod cottage in the north of Ireland," replied Mr. Fraser. "There, with my Bible open before me, I used to kneel for hours at a time, and ask the Spirit of God to reveal Christ to my soul and to open the Word to my heart. He taught me more on my knees on that mud floor than I could ever have learned in all the colleges and seminaries in the world."

Discernment

Noah was a man of discernment because he had a divine perspective, "Of things not yet seen." 2 Corinthians 5:7 says that believers walk by faith and not by sight, "The path we walk is charted by faith, not by what we see with our eyes" (The Voice Bible). As Noah was constructing the Ark, no doubt his world viewed him as a man who was going to a lot of trouble for nothing. There were no signs at all that there was coming a flood. Not only had there never been a flood before, but even rain was then unknown. At this time, the entire earth was surrounded by a canopy of mist. Earth was much like a greenhouse, watered each day by morning dew. Such an event spoken of by Noah was unprecedented, and could only happen by a miracle. Some read this, "He was forewarned of things not seen as yet." Noah had discernment, an intimation of coming judgment which he believed was from God, and to be the truth.

Spurgeon said, "God has given you 'eyes' in 'your heart.' Divine things are seen better by your heart than by your physical eyes, or your mind. When you put the telescope of faith over the eyes of your heart, you can see much more than you have ever seen."[9] In Isaiah 21:11, we read, "Watchman, what of the night? [How far is it spent? How long till morning?] Guardian, what of the night?" (The Amplified Bible) ✶ The watchman was a sentinel on an ancient city watchtower looking for any approach of danger from the enemy. Noah was much like a "watchman" because of his discernment. He was able to look more than a century into the future to see the truth of God's displeasure and warning. The Amplified Bible expresses his discernment, "Being forewarned by God concerning events of which as yet there was no a visible sign."

In Luke 12: 54 – 56, Christ reprimanded the religious leaders for their lack of discernment concerning their day. They could read the signs of good and bad weather, but could not "discern" (examine) "the day" in which they lived. On May 8, 1902, residents of the beautiful West Indies island of Martinique greeted the dawn as they had their entire lives, with no expectation of impending death and destruction. However, there was a problem. The most popular volcano, Mt. Pelee, had been acting rather strange. A month before, a volcanologist warned them that they should evacuate. Two weeks later, the crater filled with steaming sulphurous water. On May 4th, an eruption blanketed the town of St. Pierre with ash. Some did leave, but most simply cleaned up the ash, and continued their business

126

as usual. At 8:02 a. m., on May 8, the volcano exploded, instantly incinerating 28,000 residents. This was the deadliest volcano eruption of the 20th century, but could have been avoided if only they would have listened.[10] As in the days of Noah, they chose not to heed the warning of the man of discernment.

Godly Fear

Noah was a man of godly fear, "…moved with godly fear,"* meaning he was devout and acted with holy and godly reverence.* He was careful and cautious in conduct because of devotion towards God.* Noah gave careful attention to the way he conducted himself in all circumstances. Regardless of the world's opinion or ridicule, he maintained a blameless life. Five times in Ephesians, chapters four and five, Paul says, "Walk..." which speaks of a manner of conduct in life. In one of these admonitions, he says to "walk circumspectly." *This means to be careful and cautious in this life so as to please God.* Both Psalms 15 and 24 declare that those who have godly fear will "walk uprightly, work righteousness, speak the truth from the heart, with clean hands and a pure heart."

David Livingstone was a man of godly character. Henry M. Stanley found Livingstone in Africa, and lived with him for some time. Here is his testimony: "I went to Africa as prejudiced as the biggest atheist in London. But there came for me a long time for reflection. I saw this solitary old man there, and asked myself, 'How on earth does he stop here – is he cracked, or what? What is it that inspires him?' For months after we met, I found myself wondering at the old man carrying out all that was said in the Bible –'leave all things and follow Me.' But little by little, his sympathy for others became contagious; my sympathy was aroused. Seeing his piety, his gentleness, his zeal, his earnestness, and how he went about his business,*I was converted by him, although he had not tried to do it."[11]

In Genesis 6:9, we read, "Noah walked with God." He lived a life of trust and obedience to God because of his reverential heart towards God. No doubt there were men of science and learning who scorned and proclaimed the impossibility of such a flood, pronouncing Noah as a fanatic. He most likely was jeered and mocked, and was the target of scornful jokes and hurtful sarcasm. Everything in the realm of probability and experience was against him. He, no doubt, during those long and lonely years, battled discouragement, and probably even questioned himself at times. Yet, because of his reverential heart for God, he endured.

Scofield defined "the fear of the Lord" as "a phrase of the Old Testament; piety meaning reverential trust with hatred of evil."[12] Long before Cornelius was converted to Christ, he feared the Lord (Acts 10:2). Fear can be defined as the terror a man feels when in danger, or it can mean an awe and reverence a man feels in the presence of God. In the Bible, others, besides Noah, were said to have "feared God" in a reverential and devout way... Abraham (Genesis 22:12), Joseph (Genesis 39:9; 42:18), Nehemiah (Nehemiah 5:15), Job (Job 1:1, 8), and the early church (Acts 9:31).

The word "reverence" is used in the Book of Leviticus. It is from a Hebrew word that means "to fear, to be godly, indicating holiness." This is what Solomon meant when he said that the whole duty of man is to "fear God and keep His commandments" (Ecclesiastes 12:13). God's prophet warned,"Behold, I am against those who prophesy false dreams, says the Lord, and tell them, and cause My people to err by their lies and by their recklessness"*(Jeremiah 23:32). "Recklessness" means "frivolity." He is warning about those who treat lightly and scorn those things of God that are to be revered, respected, and viewed with awe. Jude warned that in the last days men who are "ungodly" will infiltrate the church. "Ungodly" means "impiety, irreverent, and wicked."[13] Actually, he is speaking of "men without reverence."

131

"Those eyes which have no fear of God before them now shall have the terrors of hell before them forever."[14]

Evidently, such irreverence greatly disturbed the renowned and late pastor of the 1800's, Charles Spurgeon. He stated, "Sometimes the manners of our people are inimical to attention; they are not in the habit of attending; they attend the chapel, but do not attend to the preacher. They are accustomed to look round at every one who enters the place, and they come in at all times, sometimes with much stamping, squeaking of boots, and banging of doors. I was preaching once to a people who continually looked around, and I adopted the expedient of saying, 'Now, friends, as it is so very interesting to you to know who comes in, and it disturbs me so very much for you to look around, I will, if you like, describe each one as he comes in, so that you may sit and look at me, and keep up at least a show of decency.'"[15] "Loose talk about the things of God proceeds from loose thinking, about the same."[16]

Preparation

Noah was a man who prepared, "Prepared an ark for the saving of his household." According to James 2:17, "Faith, if it does not have works, is dead." Immediately, Noah began to show his faith by his works. An old Scotsman operated a little rowboat for transporting passengers. One day, a passenger noticed that the good old man had carved on one oar the word, "Faith," and on the other oar the word, "Works." Curiosity led him to ask the meaning of this. The old man, being a well-balanced Christian, glad at the opportunity for testimony, said, "I will show you." Then, he dropped one oar and plied the other called Works, and they just went around in circles. Then he dropped that oar, and began to ply the oar called Faith. The little boat just went around in circles again – this time the other way round, but still in a circle. After this demonstration, the old man picked up Faith and Works, and plying both oars together, glided swiftly over the water. Explaining to his inquiring passenger, "You see, that is the way it is in the Christian life. Dead works without faith are useless, and 'faith without works is dead,' and will get you nowhere. But faith and works pulling together make for progress and success."[17]

Noah "thoroughly prepared." He prepared himself first, because he knew God had placed on him a great responsibility.*1 Kings 18:46 reads, "The hand of the Lord was on Elijah. He girded up his loins, and ran before Ahab to the entrance of Jezreel [nearly twenty miles]" (The Amplified Bible). God's prophet outran a chariot almost twenty miles! How did he do it? The phrase "girded up his loins" means that he "prepared himself." Once, a wild boar of the jungle was whetting his tusks against the trunk of a tree. A fox passing by asked him why he did this, seeing that neither hunter nor hound was near. "True," replied the boar, "but, when the danger arises, I shall have something else to do than to sharpen my weapons!"[18] "It is better to look ahead and prepare than to look back and regret."[19]

The "ark" was more than just a large boat. It speaks of that which is sacred. It is the same word used for the Ark of the

Covenant spoken of in Hebrews 9:4 and Revelation 11:19. The ark Noah built was 525 feet long, 87 feet wide, 52 ½ feet high, and was made of gopher or cypress wood, which was expensive and costly, taking many years to build. Noah made a great sacrifice to prepare for the coming deluge. We have no record that he disputed with God as to the why of the ark, nor how would it ever contain all that was to be lodged in it. Neither did he question as to how such a vessel could weather such a coming storm. His faith in God caused him to work in earnest. He lived to see his faith and preparation vindicated. He lived in unquestionable obedience to God, and, then, entered the ark while the sky was cloudless. God had spoken to him, and that was enough.

While all other human beings perished in the flood, he and his wife, his three sons and their wives, were saved.*While all of his friends and neighbors forsook him, he remained faithful in preparation, "...for the saving of his household.* According to the record, Noah convinced no one else of the coming judgment except his family. *Rev. Alan Redpath stated, "For 120 years Noah preached the Gospel; tell me, how many conversions did he get? They were his wife and family. The place where the reality of a man's religion is tested the most is in his own home.*[20]

In Psalm 101:2, David vowed, "I will walk within my house in integrity and with a blameless heart" (The Amplified Bible). Adam Clarke commented, "It is easier for most men to walk with a perfect heart in the *church*, or even in the *world*, than in their own *families*. How many are as meek as lambs among

137

others, when at *home* they are *wasps* or *tigers.*"[21]

Joshua declared, "As for me and my house, we will serve the Lord" (Joshua 24:15). When the Philippian jailor made a place in his home for Christ, his entire household got saved (Acts 16:29 – 34). Cornelius made his home a place of worship and godly living, and the members of his household were filled with the Spirit (Acts 10:33, 44 – 46). It was due to the faithful training of Lois and Eunice that God used Timothy as a faithful minister of the gospel (2 Timothy 1:5).

In Andrew Murray's family, of South Africa, eleven children grew to adulthood. Five of the sons became ministers, and four of the daughters married ministers. The next generation was even more fruitful, as ten grandsons became ministers and thirteen became missionaries. For those who search for the reason for such a contribution to the Kingdom of God will find it was a Christian home.[22]

Undeterred

Noah would not be deterred, "By which he condemned the world." 2 Peter 2:5 says he was "a preacher of righteousness," as he warned with a heart of great concern. "Condemned" does not mean by a harsh and judgmental attitude, but by a righteous life. His walk of faith was a silent rebuke to the lives of the ungodly. "Condemned" has the thought of intensity, calling into question, distinguishing, and to decide mentally and judicially. This means that Noah made up his mind to distinguish between right verses wrong, and to do so with intensity, being undeterred. His life of living blamelessly was a witness against their sin. People who set a godly example will either convert the unsaved... or condemn them. Regardless of the world's opinion and ridicule of him, he continued on, and persevered to walk with God. He held tightly to the word God had given him with tenacity and perseverance. Genesis 6:9 can be read, "This is the record of Noah. Noah did what was right, remained uncontaminated in a contaminated world (and) he walked with God."

In Ezekiel 22:30, God said that He was looking for a man to "stand in the gap before Me for the land." It speaks of a person resolute enough to be willing to expose himself for the protection of something. It also means to defend against danger. Such a person builds a wall against the flood of evil. Williams Jennings Bryon, who once ran for the Presidency of the United States, was not afraid of standing against the evils of the majority when it was more popular to compromise his convictions. He wrote, "Never be afraid to stand with the minority when you feel the minority is right, for the minority which is right will one day be the majority; always be afraid to stand with the majority which is wrong, for the majority which is wrong will one day be the minority."[23]

Martin Luther stood his ground on April 18, 1521, when confronted by the "Diet of Worms." He had been called into account for his writings. The Catholic Church considered his teachings as heresy. Luther declared that they were Holy Spirit–enlightenment to a corrupt and deceived church. At the end of his allotted time, being undeterred, he declared, "My conscience is captive to the Word of God...Here I stand!" He was promptly excommunicated. After his defense, Luther was at complete peace with his decision to persevere and not relinquish his convictions. He had the attitude of David in Psalm 118:6, "The Lord is on my side; I will not fear. What can man do to me?" Because of his determination, we have the Protestant Church today, with multitudes of millions experiencing the saving knowledge of Christ.[24] "In a question of right and wrong, never be neutral" (Theodore Roosevelt).[25]

Delivered

Noah was granted God's deliverance, "And became heir of righteousness which is according to faith." His faith in

God was richly rewarded, and brought him the highest honor of being claimed as an "heir" (child of God). He unreservedly accepted God's word to him, bravely acted on it, and, as a consequence, God delivered him and his family. Year after year, he kept building the ark and preaching righteousness (2 Peter 2:5). Unlike the others, he believed what God had told him. The result was that he became an inheritor of true righteousness which is by faith.

Spurgeon said, "Those who would be transfigured with Jesus must not be disfigured by conformity to this world."[26] The Amplified Bible reads, "And became heir and possessor of righteousness (that relation of being right into which God puts the person who has faith)." Noah not only preached righteousness, but he lived it. A righteous man is one who is right with God in a practical way, whose conduct is pleasing in God's sight. In Luke 1:75, we see that the purpose of Christ's coming was that we may serve God "in holiness and righteousness." Holiness refers to character, and righteousness refers to conduct. Such a person will experience God's deliverance in this world... and at the end of the world, as did Noah.

Christ promised the believers at Philadelphia, "Because you have kept My commandments to persevere, I also will keep you from the hour of trial which shall come upon the whole world to test those who dwell on the earth" (Revelation 3:10). Vance Havner, in his book *Repent or Else!*, wrote, "G. Campbell Morgan says, 'Its final fulfillment will undoubtedly be realized

144

by those who, loyal to His word, and not denying His name, shall be gathered out of the world at His second coming before the judgment that must usher in the setting up of His kingdom on the earth.' There are two 'keeps' here. Because they kept the word of His patience, He will keep them. They kept and are kept."[27]

Conclusion

A day of reckoning is coming. In his book, *The Appointment in Samarra*, John O'Hara tells the story of the self-destruction of Julian English, once a member of the social elite of Gibbsville (O'Hara's fictionalized version of Pottsville, Pennsylvania). He tells of the legend from the streets of Bagdad of a wealthy merchant, and how he sent his servant to the market to purchase provisions. Soon, however, the servant returned empty-handed, filled with fear. He told his master how he had been jostled by a woman in the crowd, and when he turned, he saw it was Death. He said, "She looked at me and made a threatening gesture. Lend me your horse, and I will flee from this city and avoid my fate. I will go to Samarra, and there Death will not find me." The merchant lent his horse to him, and the servant fled immediately to Samarra as fast as possible. That afternoon, the master himself went to the marketplace, and he saw Death standing in the crowd. He approached her, and asked, "Why did you make a threatening gesture to my servant when you saw him this morning?' Death answered, "That was not a threatening gesture. It was only an expression of surprise. I was astonished to see him in Bagdad, for I have an appointment with him this evening in Samarra!"[1]

"Just as mortals are appointed to die once and then to experience a judgment, so the Anointed One, *our Liberating King,* was delivered once *in death* to bear the sins of many and will appear a second time, not to deal again with sin, but to rescue those who eagerly await His return" (Hebrews 9:27, 28 – The Voice Bible).

"God's darkest threatenings are always accompanied with a revelation of the way to escape. The ark is always along with the Flood" (Alexander Maclaren).[2]

References

Introduction

1. https://psalms23.blogspot.com/200
   7_05_01_archive.html

Chapter One

1. "As it Was in the Days of Noah,"
   by Ralph L. Williams, Decision
   Magazine, Billy Graham
   Association, Minneapolis, MN,
   May 1974
2. *Strong's Exhaustive Concordance
   of the Bible,* James Strong, S.T.D.,
   LL.D., Royal Publishers, Inc.,
   Nashville, TN, 37203, A
   Concise Dictionary of the Words
   in the Greek Testament, #'s
   458 and 459, p. 12
3. *A Complete Treasury of Stories for
   Public Speakers,* by Morris
   Mandel, Jonathan David
   Publishers, Middle Village, NY,
   11379, Copyright 1974, pp. 405 –
   406
4. www.special-
   dictionary.com/proverbs/keywords
   /white/

5. A. James Rudin, Religious News Service, St. Pete Times, St. Petersburg, FL, Saturday, Feb. 15, 1997

6. *Christian Clippings,* P. O. Box 3867, Holiday, FL, 34692, June 1997

7. *The Gospel of Matthew,* Volume One (Chapters 1 to 10), Revised Edition, by William Barclay, The Westminster Press, Philadelphia, PA, Copyright 1975, p. 350

8. *Strong's Exhaustive Concordance of the Bible,* James Strong, S.T.D., LL.D., Royal Publishers, Inc., Nashville, TN, 37203, Dictionary of the Hebrew Bible, #'s 2554, 2555, 7843, pp. 40 and 115

9. *Emotions: Can You Trust Them,* Dr. James Dobson, pp. 65, 66 – www.amazon.com

10. *The Prophets Mantle,* by George W. Truett, D.D., LL.D., pp. 84, 85– www.amazon.com/Prophets-Mantle-George-W-Truett/.../...

11. *Knight's Master Book of New Illustrations,* by Walter B. Knight, Wm. B. Eerdmans Publishing Company, Grand Rapids, MI,

Copyright 1956, p. 380

12. *The Youth Teacher,* Volume 1, No. 2, April – May – June, 1955, The Gospel Publishing House, Springfield, MO, 65802

13. *Robust in the Faith, Men from God's School,* J. Oswald Sanders, Moody Press, Chicago, p. 126

14. *Matthew Henry Commentary,* Genesis, pp. 53, 54 – https://www. biblegateway.com/.../mathew-henry/Gen...

15. *Pulpit Helps,* Chattanooga, TN: AMG International, August 2004

16. *Follow Thou Me,* George W. Truett, D. D., LL.D., Harper & Brothers Publishers, New York, Copyright 1932, p. 119

17. www.hcbc.com/templates/ System/ details.asp?28485&PID= 269459

18. *World Aflame,* Billy Graham, Word Publishing, Waco, TX, 1965

19. *The Treasury of David,* C. H. Spurgeon, Volume One, Psalms 1 – 57, Hendrickson Publishers, Inc., P. O. Box 3473, Peabody, MA, 01961-3473, p. 123

1. *What on Earth's Going to Happen?*, Ray C. Steadman, 1967, p. 144 – www.amazon.com/What-On-Earths-Going-Happen/.../...

2. William Barclay, *Adult Teacher Supplement,* Gospel Publishing House, Springfield, MO, Copyright 1966, p. 11

3. "Ready And Waiting," by Dan G. McCartney, Decision Magazine, Billy Graham Association, Minneapolis, MN, December 1997, pp. 31, 32

4. *In Times Like These,* Vance Havner, Fleming H. Revell Company, Old Tappan, NJ, Copyright 1969, p. 15

5. *Matthew Henry Commentary, Matthew, p. 363* – https://www.biblegateway.com/.../mathew-henry/Gen...

6. *What on Earth's Going to Happen*?, Ray C. Steadman, 1967, – www.amazon.com/What-On-Earths-Going-Happen/.../...

7. *Against the Night, Living in the Dark Ages,* Charles Colson with Ellen Santilli Smith, p. 6 –

www.barnesandnoble.com/...
against- the- night.../100201...

8. *A Complete Treasury of Stories for Public Speakers,* Morris Mandel, Jonathan David Publishers, Middle Village, NY, 11379, Copyright 1974, p. 103

9. *Against The Night, Living in the Dark Ages,* Charles Colson with Ellen Santilli Smith, p. 43 – www.barnesandnoble.com/.../ against-the-night.../100201...

10. "Future Shock," Editorial, Decision Magazine, Billy Graham Association, Minneapolis, MN, June 1973

Chapter Three

1. *Knight's Master Book of New Illustrations,* by Walter B. Knight Wm. B. Eerdmans Publishing Company, Grand Rapids, MI, Copyright 1956, p. 605

2. *Word Meanings in the New Testament,* Ralph Earle, Hendrickson Publishers, Inc., P. O. Box 3473, Peabody, MA, 01961-3473, Copyright 1974, p. 22

3. *Re-Entry,* John Wesley White,

pp. 23, 24 www.amazon.com/
Re-Entry-John-Wesley-
White/.../088...

4. Decision Magazine, Billy Graham
   Evangelistic Association,
   Minneapolis, MN, April 1998,
   pp. 31, 32

Chapter Four

1. Decision Magazine, August
   1992, p. 2
2. *The Treasury of David,* C. H.
   Spurgeon, Volume One, Part 2,
   Psalm 27 to 57, Hendrickson
   Publishers, Inc., P. O. Box 3473,
   Peabody, MA, 01961-3473, p.
   305
3. *Word Meanings in the New
   Testament,* Ralph Earle,
   Hendrickson Publishers, Inc.,
   P. O. Box 3473, Peabody, MA,
   01961-3473,
   Copyright 1974, p. 137
4. *Knight's Master Book of New
   Illustrations,* Walter B. Knight,
   Wm. B. Eerdmans Publishing
   Company, Grand Rapids, MI,
   Copyright 1956, p. 283
5. "Conscience: The Celestial Fire,"
   by G. W. Hardcastle II, The
   Pentecostal Evangel, Gospel

Publishing House, Springfield, MO, 65802, July 28, 1991

6. Ibid
7. *No Wonder They Call Him Savior,* Max Lucado, p. 146 – www.barnesandnoble.com/.../ no-wonder- they-call-him...
8. *In Times Like These,* Vance Havner, Fleming H. Revell Company, Old Tappan, NJ, Copyright 1969, pp. 127 – 12
9. *Christian Clippings,* P. O. Box 3867, Holiday, FL, 34692, May 2007, p. 20
10. "Humanism and the Holy Spirit," Amos O. Millard, Paraclete, Gospel Publishing House, Springfield, MO, Winter 1982, Volume 16, # 1, p. 5
11. "The Right to be Human," Morris Williams, The Pentecostal Evangel, Springfield, MO, 65802, October 24, 1982, p. 5
12. *Word Meanings in the New Testament,* Ralph Earle, Hendrickson Publishers, Inc., P. O. Box 3473, Peabody, MA, 01961-3473, Copyright 1974, p. 139
13. "Turning the Grace of God into Lasciviousness," David

Wilkerson, Times Square Church
Pulpit Series, New York,
August 27, 2001

14. *Against the Night, Living in the
Dark Ages,* Charles Colson with
Ellen Santilli Vaugn, p. 63 –
www.barnesandnoble.com/.../
against-the- night.../100201...

15. "Homosexuality," by Bob
Sutton, New Wine
Magazine, June 1971, p. 23

16. *Adult Teacher Supplement,* First
Quarter, The Gospel Publishing
House, Springfield, MO,
Copyright 1969, p.10

Chapter Five

1. *The Hole in the Gospel,* Richard
Stearns, Thomas Nelson, Inc.,
Nashville, TN, 2009, 2010, by
World Vision, p. 64

2. *Knight's Master Book of New
Illustrations,* Walter B. Knight,
Wm. B. Eerdmans Publishing
Company, Grand Rapids, MI,
Copyright 1956, pp. 606– 607

3. *Just a Preacher,* by Vance
Havner, Moody Press, Chicago,
IL, 1981, The Moody Bible
Institute, p. 68

4. *Strong's Exhaustive Concordance of the Bible,* James Strong, S.T.D., LL.D, Royal Publishers, Inc., Nashville, TN, 37203, A Concise Dictionary of the Words in the Greek Testament, #'s 5532, 5536, 5537, p. 78
5. Ibid – Dictionary of the Hebrew Bible, #'s 3245, 5475, pp. 50 and 82
6. *Christian Clippings,* P. O. Box 3867, Holiday, FL, 34692, February 2007, p. 23
7. "The Only Hope in the Coming Storm," by David Wilkerson, Times Square Church Pulpit Series, New York, October 3, 2011, p. 3
8. *Knight's Master Book of New Illustrations,* Walter B. Knight, Wm. B. Eerdmans Publishing Company, Grand Rapids, MI, Copyright 1956, p. 486
9. *Spurgeon's Commentary on Great Chapters of the Bible,* Tom Carter, Kregel Publications, Grand Rapids, MI, Copyright 1998, P. O. Box 2607, p. 294
10. *Pulpit Helps,* Chattanooga, TN:

AMG Publications, October
2003

11. *Knight's Master Book of New
Illustrations,* by Walter B.
Knight, Wm. B. Eerdmans
Publishing Company, Grand
Rapids, MI,
Copyright 1956, pp. 74, 75

12. *The Teen Teacher,* Volume
XXII, October, November,
December, 1953, No. 4, Gospel
Publishing House, Springfield,
MO, p. 67

13. *Strong's Exhaustive
Concordance of the Bible,* James
Strong, S.T.D., LL.D., Royal
Publishers, Inc., Nashville, TN,
37203, A Concise Dictionary of
the Words in the Greek
Testament, #'s 763, 764, 765,
p. 16

14. *The Treasury of David,* C. H.
Spurgeon, Volume One, Part
Two, Psalms 27 – 57,
Hendrickson Publishers, Inc.,
P. O. Box 3473,
Peabody, MA, 01961-3473,
p. 156

15. *Lectures to My Students,* The
Pastors College, Metropolitan
Tabernacle, by President

Charles Spurgeon, The Old
Time Gospel Hour, Lynchburg,
VA, p. 139

16. *Christian Clippings,* P. O. Box
3867, Holiday, FL, 34692,
January 1996, p. 17

17. *Knight's Master Book of New
Illustrations,* Walter B. Knight,
Wm. B. Eerdmans Publishing
Company, Grand Rapids, MI,
Copyright 1956, p. 195

18. *A Complete Treasury of Stories
for Public Speakers,* Morris
Mandel, Jonathan David
Publishers, Middle Village, NY,
11379,   Copyright 1974, p. 306

19. *Christian Clippings,* P. O. Box
3867, Holiday, FL, 34692,
February 1999

20. *Knight's Master Book of New
Illustrations,* by Walter B.
Knight, Wm. B. Eerdmans
Publishing Company, Grand
Rapids, MI,
Copyright 1956, p. 298

21. *The Treasury of David,* C. H.
Spurgeon, Volume Two (Part 2),
Psalm 88 – 110, Hendrickson
Publishers, Inc., P. O. Box 3473,
Peabody, MA, 01961-3473, p.
245

22. *Knight's Master Book of New Illustrations,* Walter B. Knight, Wm. B. Eerdmans Publishing Company, Grand Rapids, MI, Copyright 1956, p. 300

23. *A Complete Treasury of Stories for Public Speakers,* Morris Mandel, Jonathan David Publishers, Middle Village, NY, 11379, Copyright 1974, p. 293

24. *Pulpit Helps,* Chattanooga, TN: AMG International, November 2006, p. 28

25. *Christian Clippings,* P. O. Box 3867, Holiday, FL, 34692, May 1998

26. *The Treasury of David,* C. H. Spurgeon, Volume One, Psalm 1 to 57, Hendrickson Publishers, Inc., P. O. Box 3473, Peabody, MA, 01961- 3473, p. 417

27. *Repent or Else!,* Vance Havner, Fleming H. Revell Co., Westwood, NJ, Copyright MCMLVIII, p. 73

Conclusion

1. www.kstate.edu/english/baker/...
   Maugham-AS.h...
2. *Pulpit Helps*, Chattanooga, TN:
   AMG International, January
      1997

Other Titles by David R. Arnold

Discipleship Manual

Why Do Bad Things Happen
to Good People?

When You Don't Know What to Do

60 Seconds January – June

60 Seconds July – December

A Church or A Courthouse

Daniel   The Most High Rules in the
Affairs of Men

What Will the End Be?
The Book of Revelation

Journey of the Patriarchs (Genesis)

Journey of the Patriarchs Workbook

To Contact:
davidarnoldministries@gmail.com

Made in the USA
Charleston, SC
16 April 2016